HENRY PURCELL

HENRY PURCELL

1658 - 1695

BY

DR. WILLIAM H. CUMMINGS

FOREWORD BY
FRANCESCO BERGER
HON. R.A.M., F.G.S.M.

HASKELL HOUSE PUBLISHERS LTD.
Publishers of Scarce Scholarly Books
NEW YORK, N. Y. 10012
1969

First Published 1881

HASKELL HOUSE PUBLISHERS Ltd.
Publishers of Scarce Scholarly Books
280 LAFAYETTE STREET
NEW YORK, N. Y. 10012

Library of Congress Catalog Card Number: **68-25285**

Standard Book Number 8383-0285-8

Printed in the United States of America

PUBLISHERS' ANNOUNCEMENT

TAKE the light away from the skies, take the flowers off our earth, take the waves from the sea, and take Music out of our lives, and what is left ?   A darkened world, a barren earth, a waste of stagnant water, saddened days and joyless nights.

Music, in one form or another,—whether learned or simple, vocal or instrumental, dramatic or lyrical, appeals to our entire race, and those who have spent their years in producing it for us, have contributed abundantly to the sum of human happiness. Acknowledging our indebtedness to them, it is but natural that we should wish to know something about the when, where, and how, of their activities.

This information the present series of biographies of Music's mighty Masters, supplies, in briefly-told volumes, full of reliable facts, with very little exaggeration or partisanship, and compiled by authors of highest standing, each with special qualification for his task.

The volumes are issued at the uniform price of 2s. 6d., and are obtainable from any bookseller in the Kingdom and Colonies.

The general editorship has been entrusted to Mr. Francesco Berger, Hon. R.A.M., F.G.S.M., whose extended experience has been of valuable service to us and whose ready help we gratefully acknowledge.

SAMPSON LOW, MARSTON & CO., LTD.

PURCELL

WE have every reason to feel grateful to the late Dr. W. H. Cummings for his interesting and informing biography of Purcell—one of the brightest stars in the musical firmament, and a man who so largely helps to dispel the false charge of our not being a musical nation.

It is unquestionable that this country has not, in the past, produced so many great Composers of opera or symphony as other countries. The vogue for Italian opera, and its resultant importation of Italian artists, and the absorption of our manhood's energies in wars with America and France, in successful colonisation, and in commercial enterprise, have contributed to this condition.

Still, with a Purcell, an Arne, a Sterndale Bennett, a Sullivan, a Balfe, a Wallace, and some others, not to name the brilliant array of our church-music and madrigal Composers, though we have not eclipsed other nations, we have at least honourably competed with them. And the race of our living Composers promises that we shall, in the near future, regain the pre-eminence we enjoyed in the days of Purcell.

In his preface to the original edition of this volume, the editor, Dr. W. H. Cummings, says: "My hope is that this little work may be the forerunner of other Purcell studies, giving further details respecting Purcell's ancestry, descendants, and family, and also saying something more of his noteworthy contemporaries and pupils." This wish I heartily share.

F. B.

PURCELL.

MUSIC and poetry attained to a high state of culti-
vation in the reign of Elizabeth; the Queen herself
was an admirable performer on the virginals, and by
her example and authority did all that was possible
to elevate the art of music, and to encourage learned
musicians throughout her dominions. This happy
condition of things was continued by her successors,
James I. and Charles I., but with the establishment
of the Commonwealth all music, both of church and
theatre, was rigidly suppressed. We read with horror
and indignation of the wanton destruction of church
organs and other musical instruments, and of the tear-
ing and burning of the various Service-books which had
been in use in the cathedrals and collegiate establish-
ments. At Canterbury cathedral " the soldiers violated
the monuments of the dead, spoyled the organs, broke
down the ancient rails and seats with the brazen
eagle which did support the Bible, forced open the
cupboards of the singing-men, rent some of their sur-
plices, gowns, and Bibles, and carryed away others,
mangled all our Service-books and books of Common

Prayer, bestrewing the whole pavement with the leaves thereof." At Rochester cathedral, Colonel Sands, hearing the organs, cryed, " *A devil on those bag-pipes*," and "one of the rebels" discharged a pistol at the head of Prebend Larken, who interposed and endeavoured to prevent the spoliation of the cathedral. At Chichester cathedral, the officers having sacked the plate and vestments, left the "destructive and spoyling part to be finished by the common soldiers, who brake down the organs, and dashing the pipes with their pole-axes, scoffingly said, '*Hark how the organs go !*' They force open all the locks, either of doors or desks wherein the singing-men laid up their Common Prayer books, their singing-books, their gowns and surplesses; they rent the books in pieces, and scatter the torn leaves all over the church, even to the covering of the pavement." At Winchester "They enter the church with colours flying, their drums beating, their matches fired, and that all might have their part in so horrid an attempt, some of their troops of horse also accompanied them in their march, and rode up through the body of the church and quire until they came to the altar; there they begin their work ; they rudely pluck down the table and break the rail, and afterwards carrying it to an ale-house they set in on fire, and in that fire burnt the books of Common Prayer and all the singing-books belonging to the Quire; they throw down the organ and break the stories of the Old and New Testament curiously cut out in carved work. The troopers ride through the streets in surplesses, carrying Common Prayer books and some broken organ pipes."

In Westminster Abbey, in 1643, " Soldiers were quartered who brake down the rail about the altar, and burnt it in the place where it stood ; they brake down the organ and pawned the pipes at several ale-houses for pots of ale; they put on some of the singing-men's surplesses, and in contempt of that canonical habit, ran up and down the church ; he that wore the surpless was the hare, the rest were the hounds."

It would be needless to add to these miserable stories ; those who care to read further on the subject, are referred to the quaint old book *Mercurius Rusticus*, from whence the foregoing extracts have been taken.

So complete was the destruction of church music-books, that examples of the pre-Commonwealth time are now most rare.

Not only were the organs and music destroyed, but musicians, organists, and singers were turned adrift, and had to seek precarious livelihoods by teaching music to the few who cared or were willing to learn the art, or else to escape starvation by adopting some less congenial occupation than that for which they were fitted by nature and education.

If tradition may be relied on, the Protector, Cromwell, was himself a lover of music, and not unwilling, when opportunity served, to assist and befriend musicians.

Cromwell's secretary, the poet Milton, was no mean performer on the organ, and being the son of an eminent composer,[1] would doubtless, with his passionate

[1] John Milton the father of the poet was the author of a six-part madrigal, "Fayre Oriane in the Morne," printed in 1601,

love for music, be at all times ready to use his sympathetic voice and counsel on behalf of any distressed and poor musician who might petition the Protector for help or redress.

It is well known that the organ which stood in Magdalen College, Oxford, was saved from destruction through the intervention of Cromwell, who privately caused it to be removed to Hampton Court, where it was placed in the great gallery, in order that he might have the frequent pleasure of hearing it; and he also appointed as his organist and music-master, at a salary of 100*l.* per annum, John Hingston, who had been one of the musicians to Charles I. Cromwell was extremely partial to the Latin *Motets* composed by Richard Dering, and these were performed on the organ by Hingston, who was assisted by his pupils in the vocal parts. The interesting organ which must have often poured forth its sweet sounds under the fingers of Milton, was, after the Protector's death, returned to Magdalen College; but subsequently the College authorities sold it, and it was removed to Tewkesbury Abbey, where it now stands.

Anthony Wood, who lived during the Protectorate, tells the following characteristic anecdote of Cromwell :—

" In October, 1659, James Quin, M.A., and one of the senior students of Christ Church, a Middlesex man

of four motets in Leighton's "Tears or Lamentacions" (1614), and of several Psalm tunes. He also composed an " In Nomine " in forty parts, for which he received a gold medal and chain from a Polish prince.

born, but son of Walter Quin, of Dublin, died in a
crazed condition. A. W. had some acquaintance
with him, and hath several times heard him sing,
with great admiration. His voice was a bass, and he
had a great command of it. 'Twas very strong and
exceeding *trouling*, but he wanted skill, and could
scarce sing in consort. He had been turned out of
his student's place by the visitors, but being well
acquainted with some great men of those times that
loved music, they introduced him into the company
of Oliver Cromwell, the Protector, who loved a good
voice and instrumental music well. He heard him
sing with very great delight, liquored him with
sack, and in conclusion, said: ' *Mr. Quin, you have
done very well, what shall I do for you ?* ' To which
Quin made answer, with great compliments, of which
he had command, with a great grace, that ' *Your
Highness would be pleased to restore him to his student's
place*,' which he did accordingly, and so kept it to his
dying day."

It must not be forgotten that although during the
Commonwealth musicians found it difficult to earn
their bread in consequence of the prohibition of all
public exhibition of their executive skill, yet many of
the learned and erudite musical treatises which have
been handed down to us were published at that time.
From this we may be sure that the musical predilections
of Cromwell were regarded with secret hope by the few
musicians who were able privately to pursue their
calling; and indeed public signs were not wanting
during the latter years of the Protector's life, that
had he been spared, the art of music would probably
have received more emphatic and distinct assistance

at his hands. In 1656 he granted a licence to Sir
William Davenant to open a kind of theatre [1] for "an
entertainment in declamation and music after the manner of the ancients;" and later on he licensed certain
theatrical performances at the Cockpit, in Drury Lane.

The extreme Puritan party did, however, so effectually
destroy and put down all Church music,[2] deeming organs
and service-books superstitious and ungodly, that at the
Restoration, when the authorities set about re-estab-
lishing musical services in the cathedrals, it was impos-
sible to find either instruments, books, or singers
necessary for the purpose; and, indeed, out of the
large musical establishment of Charles I., only three
men—Dr. Wilson, Christopher Gibbons, and Henry
Lawes—came forward at the Restoration to claim their
former appointments.

We get a further insight into the condition of Church
music at the Restoration, from Matthew Locke's *Present
Practice of Musick Vindicated*, published in 1673,
wherein he says, "For above a year after the opening
of His Majestie's Chappel, the orderers of the musick
there were necessitated to supply superior parts of the
music with cornets and men's feigned voices, there
being not one lad for all that time capable of singing
his part readily."

---

[1] In a room behind Rutland House, Aldersgate Street.
[2] "Instrumental and Cathedral music I have ever been wilfully
ignorant of, because I have dearly loved them, and if I had
learnt them to a perfection, this satiety might have bred a
nauseous distaste and surfeit, as in other things, and then I had
nothing to delight in. But alas! this conceit hath failed me,
*for now all church music my highest terrene content is abandoned
amongst us.*"—PHILIP KING's "Surfeit," 1656.

An examination of the old MS. copies of anthems composed by the organists and singing-men of the various cathedrals in the reign of Charles II., shows that a dearth of singing-boys (trebles) was general throughout the kingdom, the compositions being chiefly for men's voices only.

From the preceding slight and brief sketch of the state of music during the Commonwealth, it will be evident that the Puritan rule was most unpropitious for the art; with its professors banned, and its public performance well-nigh extinguished, music might perhaps have been expected to have died an unnatural death; but heaven-born, it retained a vital spark which needed only the breath of freedom and gentle encouragement to foster it into a flame.

With the death of Cromwell, the sun of the Puritan world vanished, but happily at the same time a new star in the musical firmament arose. Cromwell died in 1658, at Whitehall, and in the same year, within a bow-shot of the Palace, was born the favoured child of the muses, destined to raise the musical fame of England to a height it had never before attained, and by his beautiful creations to make for himself a name of undying fame.

This welcome prodigy was Henry Purcell, his birthplace St. Ann's Lane, Old Pye Street, Westminster. The precise day of his birth there is unknown, but there is no doubt about the year 1658. Some remains of the house are still standing. A sketch of it and the adjoining premises was made on the 15th of April, 1845, by R. W. Withall.

The original drawing, of which a reduced copy is given, has the following note :—

"Three ancient houses in Westminster; in the right-hand one of which the great H. Purcell was born, 1658, and passed his early life. They are now in the last state of ruin, and have long been uninhabited. The houses adjoining that of Purcell are of modern date, and project before the others, as well as encroach somewhat on Purcell's doorway, hiding

PURCELL'S HOUSE.

one side of the door-frame. Of the old houses the windows and doorways are nearly all boarded up in the roughest manner, under which, however, the original panelled doors are still to be partly found. The houses are of old red brick. The first door was the back way into the public-house called the 'Bell and Fish,' kept by Mr. Oldsworth, who lost his licence. The second door the entrance to the skittle-ground. The third was Purcell's house."

Purcell was named Henry after his father, a thoroughly competent and efficient musician, of whom Pepys made this quaint entry in his diary on the 21st of February, 1659 :—

" After dinner I back to Westminster Hall with him (Mr. Crewe) in his coach. Here I met with Mr. Lock and Pursell, masters of musique, and with them to the Coffee House, into a room next the water, by ourselves, where we spent an hour or two, till Captain Taylor came and told us that the House had voted the gates of the city to be made up again, and the members of the city that are in prison to be set at liberty; and that Sir G. Booth's case be brought into the House to-morrow. Here we had variety of brave Italian and Spanish songs, and a canon for eight voices, which Mr. Lock had lately made on these words, ' Domine salvum fac Regem,' — an admirable thing. Here out of the window it was a most pleasant sight to see the city from one end to the other with a glory about it, so high was the light of the bonfires, and so thick round the City ; and the bells rang everywhere."

We may note here the intimacy which existed between Purcell's father and Matthew Locke,[1] the celebrated composer, an intimacy and friendship which was afterwards extended to the son.

Henry Purcell, senior, was a gentleman of the Chapel Royal, and in that capacity sang in the choir at the coronation of Charles II.[2] He was also elected a singing-man of Westminster Abbey, and master of the

[1] They acted together in "The Siege of Rhodes " in 1656.
[2] His name appears in the cheque-book of the Chapel Royal as Henry *Purcill*, and from the same source we learn that

B

chorister boys of that church ; to these appointments he added that of music copyist of Westminster Abbey, at that time a very honourable and important position, in consequence of the wholesale destruction of Service-books which had taken place during the Common-wealth.

A very interesting official document, now pre-served in the British Museum, of which the follow-ing is a copy, gives us information respecting the appointments held by Henry Purcell, the father, in Westminster Abbey :—

"Accounts of Richard Busby, D.D., 1664. The money computed by John Needham (Gent.) receiver of the college.

" Cantator in choro Henry Purcell £8 and 40s.
In ᵗᵒ· chorist Henry Purcell £10.
Cantator in choro per stipend et regard—
John Harding, Christopher Chapman,
Henry Purcell, Edwd. Braddock,
William Hutton, Owen Adamson,
Thomas Hughes, Peter Amblett, Thomas Shorter,
Thomas Condy, Thomas Finnell—each £8 and 40s.

" Choristicus—
Et in denariis solutis Henry Purcell,
Pro datum chorist ad—lxviˢ viyᵈ
Intoto hoc anno   xxxiy£ viˢ viyᵈ.
Ac etiam et contess Hen°· Purcell, pro
Chorist.   xx£.
Organista Chr. Gibbons £10.

he, in common with the other gentlemen of the Chapel, received (each of them), four yards of fine scarlet cloth for a gown to wear at the coronation.

" To Mr. Chaunter for nine Holly days—

			£	s.
On All Saints day	39s.			
The first of November	„			
Christmas day	„			
Epiphany	„			
Candlemas day	„		8	12
Lady day	„			
Easter day	„			
Whitson day	„			
St. Peter's day	„			

" To George Dalham, for tuning the organ this year, 40s.[1]

" To John Hill,[2] for playing on the cornett in the church this year, £4.

" To the organist for rent of his house, £8.

" Given to the organist[3] out of the rents at the taking of his degree, £5.

" Given by order to the christened Turke—nil.[4]

" Jan. 11, 1664—" J. DOLBEN, *Decanus.*
    WAL. JONES, *Sub Decanus.*
    H. KILLIGREW.
    S. BOLTON.
    CHARLES GIBBES.
    ROBT. SOUTH.
    RIC. PERRINCHIEF."

[1] George Dalham, a well-known organ builder. Dr. Rimbault says Father Smith built the organ erected in West[r] Abbey at the Restoration, but this payment would suggest a doubt as to his accuracy.

[2] Hill played the treble parts on the cornet in consequence of the difficulty previously mentioned, of obtaining efficient boys. He was buried in the cloisters of W. A., in 1667.

[3] Christopher Gibbons, son of the celebrated Orlando Gibbons, was organist of Winchester Cathedral in the reign of Charles I., but on the breaking out of the civil war he became a soldier. He was admitted Doctor of Music at Oxford, by the special desire of Charles II.

[4] Where the word "nil" now stands in the MS. there has evidently been an erasure of some figure or figures.

In addition to the before-mentioned appointments at the Chapel Royal and Westminster Abbey held by Purcell, senior, we find that he was also a member of the Royal band. The old cheque-book of the Chapel Royal in recording his death places the matter beyond doubt :—

"These are to certify that Mr. Henry Purcell, who succeeded Segnor Angello in his place of the private musicke; that the said Mr. Henry Purcell took possession of his place in the year 1663, upon St. Thomas's day ; deceased the 11th August, 1664. These are to certifye the death of Mr. Henry Purcell.

"HENRY COOKE.   THO. PURCELL.
ALPHONSO MARSH.   GREGORY THORNDALE.
EDWARD COLMAN."

It is clear from the foregoing account of the numerous important musical posts which the father held, that he was a man of considerable ability, and fully equal to the task of guiding and fostering the musical predilections of his infant son ; and there can be no doubt that Henry Purcell received his earliest instructions in the art of music from his father. When the latter died he was buried in the cloisters of Westminster Abbey ; his age has not been ascertained, but presumably he was but a young man—perhaps he was naturally weak in constitution—and from him the boy Henry may have inherited the seeds of consumption. The elder Purcell died in 1664, at which time the young Henry was just six years old, and with his natural genius he had doubtless already acquired some considerable skill in music. It is certain that he was immediately admitted as a chorister of the Chapel Royal. Happily for him he had been left by his father to the guardianship of his uncle Thomas Purcell, who most warmly and affectionately endeavoured to supply the place of the lost parent by adopting the orphan as his own son.

Thomas Purcell's abilities and professional qualifications well fitted him for the task which had fallen to his lot. He was a gentleman of the Chapel Royal and had been associated with his brother Henry at the coronation of Charles II.; he must have been held in high favour and regard by the king, for court appointments in various musical capacities fell to him in rapid succession. Amongst other honourable positions we find him holding the post of lutenist as described in the following warrant:—

"Charles R., by the Grace of God, &c., to our trusty and well-beloved Sr Edward Griffin, Knight, Treasurer of our Chamber, &c. Whereas wee have made choice of Thomas Purcell to serve us in the office and place of one of our musitians in ordinary for the lute and voyce, in the roome of Henry Lawes, deceased, and for this service and attendance in that place, are pleased to allow him the wages and livery of six-and-thirty pounds two shillings and sixpence by the year during his life. Our will and pleasure is, and We do hereby will and command you to pay, or cause to be paid, unto the said Thomas Purcell or his assigns, the said wages and livery, &c. The first payment to commence and begin from the birth of our Lord, next ensuing the date hereof, and to continue the same during the natural life of him, the said Thomas Purcell. Given the 29th of November, in the 14th year of our reign (1662). "Ex. pr. WARWICK."

In 1672 Thomas Purcell was appointed a " composer in ordinary for the violins " in conjunction with Pelham Humphries, the warrant which is extremely curious runs thus :—

" Charles R., by the Grace of God, &c., to our trusty and well-beloved Sir Edward Griffin, Knight, Treasurer of our Chamber, now being, &c. Whereas we have been pleased to take into our service as Composer in Ordinary for the Violins, Thomas Purcell and Pelham Humphreys, Gents., in the room of George Hudson, deceased, and for their entertainments in consideration of services done, and to be done, unto us, we have given and granted, and by these presents do for us and Our Heirs and Successors, Wee do give and grant unto the said Thomas Purcell and Pelham Humphreys for their wages and fee, the sum of fifty-two pounds fifteen shillings and tenpence, by the year, during their natural lives, and the life of the longer liver of them, the first payment to commence from the feast of St. Michael the Archangel, 1672. Given under our Signet at our Palace of Westminster, the Eighth day of August, in the year of our Lord God, One thousand six hundred and seventy-two (1672).

" Ex. JOHN NICOLAS."

Thomas Purcell and Pelham Humphries were also associated as masters of the King's band of " four-and-twenty fiddlers ; " but Purcell was chief and leader, either by virtue of seniority or special appointment.

A curious document in Thomas Purcell's autograph is preserved by the " Royal Society of Musicians," which gives the names of the gentlemen of the band and other interesting particulars ; it reads as follows :—

"The names of the Gen^t. of his Maties Private Musick who are to attend his Matie at Windsor paid out the Excheker:

	£	s.	d.
Tho. Mr. Purcell ⎫ Pelham Mr. Humphreys ⎭	200	0	0
Jo^n. Mr. Hardinge	40	0	0
W^m. Mr. Howes.	46	10	10
Tho. Mr. Blagrave, Seig^r.	40	9	2
Alphonso Mr. March.	40	0	0
Jo^n. Mr. Goodgroome . . .	40	0	0
Nat. Mr. Wattkins	40	0	0
Math. Mr. Lock	40	0	0
Jo^n. Mr. Clayton	152	13	4
Isaac Mr. Stagins, Seig^r. . . .	46	10	10
Nich. Mr. Stagings, Junr. . . .	46	10	10
Tho. Mr. Battes	90	0	0
John Mr. Lilly	40	0	0
Hen. Mr. Gregory	60	0	0
Theophilus Mr. Hills	46	10	10
Henry Mr. Madge	86	12	8
John Mr. Gombell	46	10	10
Rich^d. Mr. Dorney . . .	20	0	0
Jo^n. Mr. Banister, Seig^r. .	100	0	0
Phil. Mr. Beckett . . .	60	2	6
Ro^b. Mr. Blagrave, Junr. . .	58	14	2
John Mr. Singleton . .	46	10	10
Robt. Mr. Strange	46	10	10

"15 May, 1674. These 24 Gent. of his Maties private musick are to attend at Windsore. "T. PURCELL."

In the original of the foregoing document the Christian names were evidently prefixed after the list had been written out; the spelling of the surnames is curious; Stagins, father and son are spelt differently; another proof, if it were required, of the utter indifference to such matters at that period.

Pepys in his Diary (Dec. 19, 1666) made an entry that

"many of the musique are ready to starve, they being five years behindhand for their wages." This irregularity of payment of the "King's musique" seems to have continued, for we find in the accounts of the "Treasurer of the Chamber," the following record :—

"Paid to Thomas Pursell at xx^{li} pr. ann. for Wages, and xvj^{li} ij^s vj^d pr. ann. for a Livery, due for fower yeares and 3 quarters ended at Mic'mas, 1672.

clxxj^{li} xj^s x^d ob."

Thomas Purcell was evidently a popular man, and on the 24th of June, 1672, he was elected "Marshall of the Corporation of Musique in Westminster," in room of Captain Cooke,[1] who resigned "by reason of sicknesse." Two years later he received another court appointment from the King; a state paper preserved in the Record Office tells us that he succeeded "John Wilson, deceased, to hold during His Majesty's pleasure, with the fee of £20 per annum, payable quarterly out of the Exchequer, to commence 25th March, 1674," subscribed by warrant from the Earl of Burlington, Master of His Majesty's Household.

Another warrant under the signet gives an order to the treasurer of the chamber for the time being, "to pay unto Thomas Purcell (one of His Majesty's Musicians in Ordinary, in the place of Dr. John Wilson, deceased), the wages and fee of £20 by the day, and £16 2s. 6d. yearly for a livery, payable quarterly, from Lady-day 1674, and to continue during His Majesty's pleasure."

[1] Harl. MSS. 1911.

Thomas Purcell lived till 1682, so that he had the satisfaction of witnessing the extraordinary development of his nephew's genius, and could also rejoice to see the general recognition of his merits, and of the honourable rewards he was so rapidly acquiring. When, at last, full of years and honours, Thomas departed this life, he was buried near his brother in the cloisters of Westminster Abbey. We seek in vain for the musical compositions of either Henry (the elder) or of Thomas: with the exception of a few chants in common use in our cathedrals, nothing of their work remains to us.

When Henry Purcell, the younger, became a chorister in the Chapel Royal at six years of age, the master of the boys was Captain Henry Cooke, an old musician, who had belonged to the chapel of Charles I., but who, on the breaking out of civil war, had laid aside the peaceful art of music to engage in the rough dissonances of battle and strife, and changed his service from that of a Royal musician to become a Royalist soldier. In the latter capacity he won a captain's commission, and possibly it was not less as a reward for his devotion and bravery on behalf of his king than as a recognition of his musical ability that Charles II. appointed him " Master of the Children of the Chapel." That he was well qualified for the post can be shown by reference to the opinions of his contemporaries, and also to the numerous compositions of his still extant in manuscript.

Pepys' Diary contains frequent reference to Cooke and his compositions :—

"After sermon a brave anthem of Captain Cooke's which he himself sang, and the king was well pleased with it." (Aug. 12, 1660.)

"A poor dry sermon, but a very good anthem of Captain Cooke's afterwards." (Oct. 7, 1660.)

"To Whitehall Chapel with Mr. Childe, and there did hear Captain Cooke and his boys make trial of an anthem against to-morrow, which was brave musique." (Feb. 23, 1661.)

"Captain Cooke, Mr. Gibbons, and others of the king's musicians, were come to present my Lord with some songs and symphonys, which were performed very finely." (May 19, 1661.)

"After dinner Mr. Townsend was called upon by Captain Cooke; so we three went to a taverne hard by, and there he did give us a song or two, and without doubt he hath the best manner of singing in the world." (July 27, 1661.)

"To Whitehall Chapel, where sermon almost done, and I heard Captain Cooke's new musique. This the first day of having vialls and other instruments to play a symphony between every verse of the anthems, but the musique more full than it was last Sunday, and very fine it is. But yet I could discerne Captain Cooke to overdo his part at singing, which I never did before." (September 14, 1662.)

"We had an excellent anthem sung by Captain Cooke and another, and brave musique. . . . . After dinner to chappel again, and there had another anthem of Captain Cooke's." (May 18, 1662.)

"A most excellent anthem with symphonys between, sung by Captain Cooke." (Sept. 7, 1662.)

"Captain Cooke, and his two boys, did sing some Italian songs which, I must in a word say, I think was fully the best musique that I ever yet heard in all my life." (Dec. 21, 1663.)

Cooke composed a considerable number of pieces of music for various royal and festal occasions; one curious hymn for a ceremony in connection with a festival service of the Knights of the Garter at Windsor was accompanied by "two double sackbuts and two double courtals placed at convenient distances among the classes of the gentlemen of both choirs, to the end that all might distinctly hear, and consequently keep together both in time and tune; for one sackbut and courtal was placed before the four petty canons who begun the hymn, and the other two immediately before the prebends of the college."

Captain Cooke's services were frequently required on the stage,[1] and with his many accomplishments there is no great wonder that he became conceited. Pepys, from whom so many quotations have already been made, wrote : " A vain coxcomb he is, though he sings so well; " and this charge of vanity is supported by other evidence. A contemporary historian says : " Captain Cooke was the best musician of his time till Mr. Pelham Humphreys, one of the children of the chapel educated by himself, began to rival him, after which he died with great discontent." [2]

Cooke was buried in the cloisters of Westminster Abbey in July, 1672. During the years that he was master of the children of the chapel he had as pupils many who won for themselves distinguished names as

---

[1] Cooke performed the part of "Solyman" in *The Siege of Rhodes*, in 1656, and also composed the music for the second and third acts of the opera.

[2] Wood, M.S. Ashmole, 8568.

musicians, amongst them notably Pelham Humphreys, Wise, Blow, Turner, and Purcell.

Purcell profited by Captain Cooke's instructions for a period of eight years—from the age of six to that of fourteen, a very important time in the life of a clever boy. Historians seem to have forgotten this fact, and have been disposed to credit the whole of Purcell's musical education to Pelham Humphreys or to Dr. Blow.

During these early years Purcell had already put forth specimens of his talent for musical composition. In 1667 Playford published a little three-part song entitled, "Sweet Tyraness, I now resign," which Dr. Burney has included in his history under the supposition that it was composed by Purcell's father; but there is reason to believe that it was the composition of the boy who, at the date of publication, was nine years of age. Possibly the music was originally intended as an air or song for a single voice, as we find it published in this form in 1678, in a work called *New Ayres and Dialogues*. This collection contained five other songs by Henry Purcell.

When Purcell was eleven years old, he essayed his powers in the composition of music for a piece called "The Address of the Children of the Chapel Royal to the King, and their Master, Captain Cooke, on his Majesties Birthday, A.D. 1670, composed by Master Purcell, one of the Children of the said Chapel." [1] It is also probable that in this youthful time Purcell composed the music to *Macbeth*, now commonly associated

---

[1] A copy of this birthday Ode, in the handwriting of Pelham Humphreys, was in the possession of the late Dr. Rimbault.

with the name of Matthew Locke. That the latter did
compose music for *Macbeth* is certain, as some of it is
still in existence, but it does not bear the slightest
resemblance to that popularly known as his. In favour
of Purcell, it may be noted that the *Macbeth* music has
many Purcell-like touches; that a copy of the score in
Purcell's youthful hand is in existence ;[1] that many old
MS. copies of the music have his name attached as
composer; and that he was entitled to the credit of it
was believed by Dr. William Hayes, Dr. Philip Hayes,
Dr. Arnold, and many other eminent musicians.

The music itself is clearly an elaboration and development of a series of short movements composed by
Robert Johnson for Middleton's play of *The Witch.*[2]

It must not be forgotten that many of Purcell's
anthems now in use in our cathedrals were the product
of his youthful pen and genius whilst he was still a
pupil of Cooke. Captain Cooke, the soldier musician,
died, as previously stated, in 1672, and was succeeded
in his appointment as "Master of the Children of the
Chapel" by one whose nature, genius, and scientific
knowledge of music must have stimulated and excited
in a special manner the dawning powers of the youthful
musical company committed to his charge, and the force
of whose example must have proved of the greatest
service to Purcell. This man was Pelham Humphreys ;[3]
he had been educated in the Chapel Royal under
Captain Cooke, where his abilities and his personal

[1] In my own library.—W. H. C.
[2] Johnson's music is printed in Stafford Smith's *Musica
Antiqua.*
[3] Spelt variously, Humfrey, Humphrey, Humphries.

attractions made a strong impression on Charles II. In Nov., 1663, Pepys made the following entry in his Diary : " The anthem was good after sermon, being the fifty-first psalme, made for five voices, by one of Captain Cooke's boys—a pretty boy. And they say there are four or five of them that can do as much. And here I first perceived that the king is musicall, and kept good time with his hand all along the anthem."

The *pretty boy* was undoubtedly Pelham Humphreys. Clifford's book of anthems, published in 1664, the year after the incident just recorded, contains the words of five anthems, " composed by Pelham Humphrey, one of the Children of His Majesties Chappel ; " and in Boyce's *Cathedral Music* we find Humphreys' anthem, " Have mercy upon me," the words of which are taken from the fifty-first psalm. There can be little doubt, therefore, that this was the very anthem heard and approved by Pepys.

In 1664 the king sent Humphreys to Paris,[1] to study under Lully; and he also probably went to Italy. During his absence the king gave him an appointment as one of the Gentlemen of the Chapel Royal; and on his return to London in October, 1667, he was " sworn in " to the place. He speedily produced several new compositions, sacred and secular, by command of the king.

---

[1] The following entries are from the account of Secret Service moneys kept by Sir John Shaw :—

" 1664.   To Pelham Humphreys, to defray the charge of his journey to France and Italy, 200*l.*"

" 1665.   To Pelham Humphreys, bounty 100*l.*"

" 1666.   To Pelham Humphreys, bounty 150*l.*"

Pepys' entry in his Diary for November 15, 1667, is very quaint. He says, " Home, and there find, as I expected, Mr. Cæsar and little Pelham Humphreys, lately returned from France, and is an absolute Monsieur, as full of form and confidence and vanity, and disparages everything and everybody's skill but his own. But to hear how he laughs at all the king's musick here, at Blagrave and others, that they cannot keep time or tune, nor understand anything: and at Grebus,[1] the Frenchman, the king's master of musick, how he understands nothing, nor can play on any instrument, and so cannot compose : and that he will give him a lift out of his place, and that he and the king are mighty great." On the following day, the 16th, Pepys notes that there was a performance of Pelham Humphreys' musick given before the king at Whitehall.

That Humphreys was an admirable musician, possessed of uncommon genius, is easily discernible from the numerous compositions of his which have come down to us. He took as his models Lulli and Carissimi; but fortunately Purcell's genius was stronger and more emphatic than that of his master : had it been otherwise he would have become a mere copyist; but, as we shall hereafter see, Purcell looked to Italy for good musical models, and was not afraid to express his dislike to the frivolity of the French school.

There exists a very interesting manuscript anthem in Purcell's handwriting, which was originally composed

[1] Louis Grabut.

by Humphreys, but afterwards altered and improved by Purcell.

Poor Humphreys had but a short career, or we may be sure he would have accomplished greater things than he did. Two years before he died he married a very beautiful lady, who followed him to his grave in the cloisters of Westminster Abbey in 1674, he being only twenty-seven years of age.

Purcell was then sixteen years old, and his boy-soprano voice must have been near its breaking—perhaps it had already departed. It was, however, the good custom of the period to retain as supernumeraries of the King's Chapel any of the old boys who gave evidence of musical ability. In 1666 we find " Hen. Cooke, Thomas Purcell, and other Gentlemen of the Chapel Royal, petition on behalf of themselves, the pages of the chapel, and *boys whose voices have changed*, for payment, there being no money assigned to the treasurer of the chamber for those purposes."

Purcell therefore continued attached to the Chapel Royal, and became a pupil of Dr. John Blow, the successor to Pelham Humphreys, as " Master of the Children." That Purcell studied under Blow is certain from the inscription on Blow's monument in Westminster Abbey, where it is stated that he was " master to the famous Henry Purcell." Blow was undoubtedly the very master Purcell then needed, for he was eminent for his goodness, amiability, and moral character, and combined with those excellent qualities all the learning and experience of a sound musician. His compositions are remarkable for their melodies and the boldness of their harmonical progressions.[1] He held appointments at the Chapel Royal, Westminster Abbey, St. Paul's Cathedral, and St. Margaret's, Westminster; and it speaks strongly for his singleness of heart, and the total absence of envy and jealousy in his nature, that recognising and proclaiming the remarkable abilities of his pupils, Purcell and Jeremiah Clarke, he resigned his appointments at Westminster Abbey and St. Paul's Cathedral, in order that they might occupy those prominent and advantageous positions. This estimable man, Blow, survived his dear friend and pupil, Purcell, some years, and so became his successor at Westminster Abbey, and was eventually laid in a grave close to him, nearly beneath the organ where they had so often discoursed sweet music together.

That Blow fully estimated the genius of his pupil Purcell, there can be no doubt, since many manuscript copies of the compositions of the latter exist in the handwriting of Blow. Probably it was at the suggestion of Blow that Purcell was appointed *copyist*[2] to Westminster Abbey in 1676. He succeeded the Rev. Stephen Byng, one of the minor canons, who probably resigned the post, as he did not die till 1681. Purcell was eighteen years of age when he became copyist of Westminster Abbey; hence arose the mistake made by

---

[1] Dr. Burney is particularly severe in condemning Blow's "crudites and violations of rule," and prints four pages of examples of Blow's sins; but there can be little doubt that a musician of the present day would regard the faults as mere spots on the sun of Blow's splendid music. Those who care to see what Blow could write should look at the anthems, " I was in the Spirit," and "I beheld, and lo.''

[2] For a list of Copyists of Westminster Abbey, see p. 112.

c

Burney and Hawkins, and constantly repeated on their
authority, that Purcell was appointed *organist* of Westminster Abbey at eighteen. The office of copyist he
held for two years only.

Mention has previously been made of the music to
Macbeth as the composition of Purcell; probably the
recognition of the excellence and effectiveness of this
work induced the managers of the theatres to give him
further employment; for in 1676 we find him composing
music for at least three plays—Shadwell's *Epsom-Wells*,
Dryden's *Aurenge-Zebe*, and Shadwell's *Libertine*. The
latter contains a four-part chorus, " In these delightful,
pleasant groves," still popular with choral societies.
The whole of the music of *The Libertine* is very bold,
and would be an interesting work to revive for its
merits; it is further curious from the fact that the
libretto is founded on the same story which was long
years afterwards adopted by Mozart for his opera, *Don
Giovanni*. In 1677 Purcell wrote the music for Mrs.
Behn's tragedy, *Abdelazor*, and also the music, solo and
chorus, of an ode " On the death of his Worthy Friend,
Mr. Matthew Locke, musick composer in ordinary to His
Majesty, and Organist of Her Majesties Chappel, who
Dyed in August 1677." The words of the ode are as
follow :—

> " What hope for us remains now he is gone ?
> He that knew all the power of numbers flown ;
> Alas ! too soon ; even he
> Whose skilful harmony
> Had charms for all the ills that we endure,
> And could apply a certain cure.
> From pointed griefs he'd take the pain away ;

Even ill nature did his lyre obey,
And in kind thoughts his artful hand repay :
His layes to anger and to war could move,
Then calm the tempest they had raised with love,
And with soft sounds to gentle thoughts incline,
No passion reign'd, where he did not combine.
He knew such mystic touches, that in death
Could cure the fear, or stop the parting breath :
And if to die had been his fear
Or life his care,
He with his lyre could call,
And could unite his spirits to the fight,
And vanquish Death in his own field of night.
Pleased with some powerful Hallelujah
He, wrapp'd in the joys of his own harmonie,
Sung on, and flew up to the Deitie."

Of the intimacy which existed between Locke and
the Purcell family we had some indication in the paragraph previously quoted from Pepys, where he spoke
of Purcell's father; and that the son was on similarly
friendly terms with Locke is certain. Locke lived in
the Savoy, and from thence he penned the following
letter [1] to Purcell :—

"DEAR HARRY,—Some of the gentlemen of His
Majesties musick will honor my poor lodgings with
their company this evening, and I would have you
come and join them : bring with thee, Harry, thy last
anthem, and also the canon we tried over together at
our last meeting. Thine in all kindness,

"M. LOCKE.

"*Savoy, March 16.*"

In 1678 Purcell resigned his appointment of *Copyist*
at Westminster Abbey,[2] doubtless that he might devote
more time to study and composition. In this year he

---

[1] I am indebted to the late Dr. Rimbault for a copy of this letter.

[2] He was succeeded by the Rev. William Tucker, Minor Canon
of the Abbey, and Priest of the Chapel Royal, an excellent

produced the fine music for the masque in Shadwell's mutilation of Shakespeare's *Timon of Athens.*

In 1679 Purcell does not appear to have composed music for the theatres, but that he was deeply engrossed in his favourite occupation appears from the following very curious letter, now printed for the first time :—

"This ffor Mr. John Gostling, Chaunter of y^e quire of Canterbury Cathedral. London y^e 8th of ffeb. $\frac{9}{78}$.

"Sir, I have re^{ed} y^e favor of yours of y^e 4th with y^e in-closed for my sonne Henry : I am sorry wee are like to be without you soe long as yours mentions : but 'tis very likely you may have a summons to appeare among us sooner than you imagine : for my sonne is composing wherin you will be chiefly concern'd. However, your occasions and tyes where you are must be considered and your conveniences ever complyde withall : in ye meantime assure yourself I shall be carefull of your concern's heir by minding and refreshing our master's memory of his Gratious promis when there is occasion. My wife returns thanks for ye compliment with her servis : and pray ye give both our respects and humble services to Dr. Belk and his Lady, and beleeve ever that I am, Sir, your affectionate and humble servant,

"T. PURCELL.

"Dr. Perce is in toune but I have not seen him since. I have perform'd ye compliments to Dr. Blow, Will Turner, etc.

"F faut : and E lamy are preparing for you." [1]

composer, who died in 1689. The following entry refers to his work :—

"In moneys rec^d. and paid for secret services of Charles II."
"To Eliza Tucker, wid^o relict of W^m. Tucker, for her husband's writing in 15 books, the anthems with symphonies for King Charles the 2^{nds} use in his Chappell Royal, 15*l.*"

[1] The original of this letter is in my possession.—W. H. C.

The Rev. John Gostling, M.A., to whom the letter is addressed, was at the time a Minor Canon of Canterbury Cathedral, and was celebrated for the quality and extraordinary compass of his bass voice. It was especially for him that most of the bass solos in Purcell's anthems were written. Evelyn, in his Diary (January, 1685,) speaks of that " stupendous bass, Gosling " singing before his Majesty and the Duke.

We learn from the above interesting letter that Thomas Purcell called Henry his *son*, and we can estimate his influence with his master, Charles the Second, by the successful way in which he evidently refreshed the king's memory; for only a few days after the letter was written the " Gratious promis " was fulfilled by appointing Gosling to the Chapel Royal. On the 25th of February, $\frac{9}{78}$, Mr. John Gosling was sworn " Gentleman of his Maties Chappel extraordinary," which means that his was a special or supernumerary appointment; but a vacancy in the regular staff of the Chapel occurred almost immediately, and we find the following entry in the cheque-book : " Mr. William Tucker, gent., of his Maties Chappell Royal, departed this life the 28th day of February, 1678,[1] in whose place was admitted in ordinary Mr. John Gostling, a base from Canterbury, Master of Arts."

The postscript to the letter read in connection with the previous paragraph " my sonne is composing wherin you will be chiefly concern'd " is clearly a jocose reference to Gostling's exceptionally low voice.

Purcell not only wrote double F (F faut) and double

[1] 1678 by the old style, but 1679 by the new.

E (E lamy) for him, as in the anthem, "Behold I bring
you glad tidings," but in another anthem commencing,
"They that go down to the sea in ships," he carried the
bass solo part down to double D.

The history of the composition of the latter anthem
is somewhat remarkable :—

"Charles the Second had given orders for building
a yacht, which as soon as it was finished he named the
Fubbs, in honour of the Duchess of Portsmouth, who, we
may suppose, was in her person rather full and plump.
The sculptors and painters apply this epithet to children,
and say, for instance, of the boys of Flammengo, that
they are fubby.   Soon after the vessel was launched
the King made a party to sail in the yacht down the
river and round the Kentish coast; and to keep up the
mirth and good humour of the company Mr. Gostling
was requested to be of the number. They had got
as low as the North Foreland, when a violent storm
arose, in which the King and the Duke of York were
necessitated, in order to preserve the vessel, to hand the
sails and work like common seamen. By good provid-
ence, however, they escaped to land : but the distress
they were in made an impression on the mind of
Mr. Gostling which was never effaced. Struck with a
just sense of the deliverance, and the horror of the
scene which he had but lately viewed, upon his return
to London he selected from the Psalms those passages
which declare the wonders and terrors of the deep and
gave them to Purcell to compose as an anthem, which
he did, adapting it so peculiarly to the compass of
Mr. Gostling's voice, which was a deep bass, that hardly
any person but himself was then, or has since, been
able to sing it ; but the King did not live to hear it."

Charles the Second became extremely partial to the

singing of Gostling, and was heard to say, " You may talk as much as you please of your nightingales, but I have a *gosling* who excels them all." At another time he presented Gostling with a silver egg filled with guineas, saying, " He had heard eggs were good for the voice."

Gostling was a devoted admirer of, and a performer on, the *viol da gamba,* an instrument which Purcell detested. We can therefore readily imagine that his musical susceptibilities were frequently severely taxed by the persistent practice of his friend. He accordingly composed a round for three voices to the following words,[1] which he presented to Gostling :—

> " Of all the instruments that are,
> None with the viol can compare.
> Mark how the strings their order keep
> With a whet, whet, whet, and a sweep, sweep, sweep.
> But above all this still abounds
> With a zingle, zingle, zing, and a zit zan zounds."

In 1680 Dr. Blow magnanimously resigned the appointment of organist of Westminster Abbey in favour of Purcell,[2] who thus became possessed of one of the most distinguished musical positions in the kingdom at the early age of twenty-two.

In the same year Purcell composed the music for Lee's tragedy, *Theodosius, or the Force of Love.* It was performed at the Duke's Theatre, and the music of the songs was soon after published by Bently as an Appendix to the play. He also wrote music for D'Urfey's comedy,

---

[1] The music was published in a collection called *The Catch Club ; or, Merry Companions.*
[2] For a list of the Organists of Westminster Abbey, see p. 111.

The Virtuous Wife, and two odes, the first, addressed
to the Duke of York, entitled "An Ode or Welcome
Song for his Royal Highness on his Return from
Scotland," and the second called "A Song to Welcome
Home His Majesty from Windsor."

But the most remarkable work of Purcell in this year
(1680) was the composition of the opera *Dido and
Æneas,* usually ascribed to his seventeenth year, 1675, a
complete mistake. An original copy of the libretto still
exists, with the following title, "An Opera performed
at Mr. Josias Priest's Boarding-school at Chelsey, by
young gentlewomen, the words made by Mr. Nat. Tate.
The musick composed by Mr. Henry Purcell."

That this was the first performance is tolerably
certain, for we find in D'Urfey's *New Poems,* 1690, "An
Epilogue to the Opera of *Dido and Æneas,* performed at
Mr. Priest's Boarding-school at Chelsey: spoken by the
Lady Dorothy Burk." We know that Priest removed
to Chelsey in 1680 by an advertisement in the *London
Gazette,* November 25th, 1680: "Josias Priest, dancing-
master, who kept a boarding-school of gentlewomen in
Leicester-fields, is removed to the great school-house at
Chelsey, that was Mr. Portman's. There will continue
the same masters and others to the improvement of the
said school."

Dido and Æneas will always remain a monument
to Purcell's extraordinary genius; it is in perfect
opera form, with an entire absence of dialogue, the
whole of the libretto being set in recitative, solos,
duets, and chorus. The opera is short, yet we cannot
but recognise the fact that had there been a public

demand for absolute music-drama, or even a proper appreciation of a work cast in such a mould, the composer had arisen who possessed the necessary genius, inspiration, and feeling for building up a school of opera which would have proved a model for his own and succeeding generations, but the time was not ripe for such a development. Purcell, like many other gifted mortals, lived before his time, and thus his perfect specimen of music-drama remains unique : so far as we know he never attempted such another work.

There is a tradition that the part of Belinda (or Anna), written for alto voice, was sung and acted [1] by Purcell himself. The music of this opera remained in MS. until 1840, when it was published by the "Musical Antiquarian Society," edited by G. A. Macfarren, unfortunately from an imperfect copy of the score, the only one then attainable. It has been frequently performed since Purcell's time, notably at the "Ancient Concerts" in London, and more recently at Liverpool. In this eventful year, or the succeeding one, 1681, Purcell took unto himself a wife, and in the latter year he again composed an ode or "Welcome Song" which must have brought him favourably under the notice of the King. It commences, "Swifter Isis, swifter flow."

In July, 1682, his abilities were publicly recognised by giving him the appointment of Organist of the Chapel Royal in place of Edward Lowe, deceased. The honour

---

[1] In 1794 S. Harding published a portrait of "Henry Purcell, musician and actor," copied from the original in Dulwich College. I have made diligent search for the painting without success. —W. H. C.

and the additional income would be welcomed by the young couple just starting on the voyage of life as a favourable augury for their future comfort and prosperity.

In this same year Purcell wrote music for a grand civic festival, "The inauguration of the truly loyal and right honourable Sir William Prichard, Knight, lord Mayor of the city of London, president of the honourable Artillery Company, and a member of the worshipful company of Merchant-Taylors. Perform'd on Monday, September xxx. 1682." In the following month he composed another "Ode or Welcome Song to the King on his return from Newmarket, Oct. 21."

The old uncle, Thomas Purcell, must have been well pleased to witness his adopted son's happiness and success; of the intercourse and friendship which continued to exist between them we have evidence. When Thomas became too old to go himself to the Pay-office for his salaries he executed a power of attorney authorizing his son Matthew to act for him, and this document was witnessed by Frances Purcell—Henry's wife.

The quaint deed is worthy of reproduction here.[1] The original is in my possession.

---

[1] Know all men by these presents that I, Thomas Purcell, of the Parish of St. Martin's-in-the-Fields, in the County of Middx., one of the gentlemen of his Ma^ts Chappell Royall, and servant to his Matie, have assign'd, ordain'd, and made, by these presents doe assigne, ordayne, and make my trusty and well beloved son, Mathew Purcell, my true and lawful Attorney for me and in my name, and to my use to aske, take, and receive all such arrears and summes of money as are due, and hereafter will become due and payable to me the said Thomas Purcell out of his Ma^ts Treasury, Chamb^r Exchequer, Coffery office, or any

A few months afterwards, July 31st, 1682, the old man died, and on the 2nd of August his mortal remains were laid to rest in the cloisters of Westminster Abbey. We can easily imagine the grief of Purcell who had to mourn the loss of one who had been more than a father to him.

A few days after the funeral of the uncle Thomas, Purcell had occasion to rejoice in the birth of a son and heir; the child was baptized in Westminster Abbey, receiving the names of John Baptista, probably a mark of friendly regard for the well-known musician, John Baptist Draghi,[1] but the infant survived only a few

---

other place or office whatsomever, giving, and by these presents granting unto my s^d Attorney my whole Power and authority in and about the premises, and upon Rec^t of any such summes of money aforesaid, Acquittance, or other discharges for me and in my name to make and give, and for me and in my name to doe and performe as fully and largely in every respect to all intents and purposes as I myself might or could doe if I were there personally present, ratifying, confirming, and allowing all and whatsomever my said Attorney shall lawfully do or cause to be done in and about the premises aforesaid by Vertue of these presents. In witness whereof I have hereunto set my hand and seale, this 15th day of May in the three-and-thirtieth yeare of King Charles the Second over England, &c. Annoq. Domini 1681.   T. PURCELL.

Sealed and delivered in the
    presence of
        F. PURCELL.
    Witt. WALLEY.

[1] Giovanni Baptista Draghi, born in Italy, came to England about the middle of the 17th century, and at the death of Matthew Locke he obtained the appointment of organist to Catherine of Braganza, wife of Charles II. Draghi was in great request as a performer and teacher of the harpischord; amongst his pupils were the Princess Anne and probably her sister Mary. He was a good composer, and had by diligent

months and was buried with his kindred in the Abbey
cloisters.   There is a volume of music in the handwriting of Henry Purcell in the Fitzwilliam Library at
Cambridge, containing an entry which is worthy of note
in this place as showing the serious tone of his mind at
that period : at the end of an anthem he has written,
"God bless Mr. Henry Purcell.   September y° 10th,
1682."

In the following year Purcell ventured on his first
publication, for which he solicited subscribers. His pro-
spectus or proposals are lost, but the following advertisement from the *London Gazette*, May 24th, 1683, throws
much light on the subject :—

"These are to give Notice to all Gentlemen that have
subscribed to the Proposals Published by Mr. Henry
Purcell for the Printing his Sonata's of three Parts for
two Violins and Base to the Harpsecord or Organ, that
the said Books are now completely finished, and shall
be delivered to them upon the 11th June next : and if
any who have not yet Subscribed, shall before that time
Subscribe, according to the said Proposals (which is Ten
Shillings the whole Sett), which are at Mr. Hall's house
in Norfolk-street, or at Mr. Playford's and Mr. Carr's
shop in the Temple ; for the said Books will not after
that time be Sold under 15*s.* the Sett."

Again   on   the   following   June   the   7th, another
advertisement appeared in the *London Gazette :—*

study made himself well acquainted with the compositions of the
best English masters whose manner of composing he adopted.
He set to music an Ode written by Dryden for St. Cecilia's day,
1687, and in contemporary copies of the words we find his
name anglicised to John Baptist Draghi.

" Wheras the time is now expired, this is therefore to
desire those Persons that have subscribed to Mr. Henry
Purcels Sonata's to repair to his house in St. Ann's
Lane beyond Westminster Abbey, or to send Proposal-
Paper they received with the Receipt to it when they
Subscribed, and those who subscribed without a Paper
or Receipt to bring a Note under the Persons Hand to
whom they Subscribed, that there may be no mistake
and they shall receive their Books, paying the remainder
part of the money."

Judging by the extreme rarity of the work, the subscription list must have been a poor one, and as the
price charged was only ten shillings for the complete
work, Purcell must have been considerably out of
pocket, when he came to balance his accounts after
paying the engraver and printer; the former was the
celebrated copper-plate engraver, Thomas Cross, junior.
The title of the work reads thus: " Sonnata's of III.
parts. Two Viollins and Basse to the Organ or Harpsichord. Composed by Henry Purcell, Composer in
Ordinary to his Most sacred Majesty, and Organist of
his Chappell Royall, London. Printed for the Author,
and sold by J. Playford and J. Carr at the Temple,
Fleet St. 1683."

The sonatas are printed in four separate parts for
the instruments named, but there is no score, the first
violin part is embellished with a splendid portrait of
the composer, lettered " Vera Effigies Henrici Purcell,
Atat Suæ 24."

The dedication runs as follows:—

"To the King. May it please yor Maj^{ty}. I had not

assum'd the confidence of laying y⁰ following Compositions at your Sacred feet; but that (as they are
the immediate Results of your Majesties Royall favour,
and benignity to me which have made me what I am),
so, I am constrain'd to hope, I may presume, amongst
Others of your Majesties over-oblig'd and altogether
undeserving Subjects, that your Maj^ty will with your
accustom'd Clemency, Vouchsafe to Pardon the best
endeavours of yor Maj^ties Most Humble and Obedient
Subject and Servant,

" H. Purcell."

The modest preface is interesting from its reference
to the novel use of Italian terms, and also as showing
the comparative regard in which Italian and French
music was held by the author, who writes :—

"Ingenious Reader.   Instead of an elaborate harangue
on the beauty and the charms of Musick which (after
all the learned Encomions that words can contrive)
commends itself best by the performances of a skilful
hand, and an angelical voice : I shall say but a very
few things by way of Preface, concerning the following
Book, and its Author : for its Author, he has faithfully
endeavour'd a just imitation of the most fam'd Italian
Masters; principally, to bring the Seriousness and
gravity of that sort of Musick into vogue, and reputation among our Country-men, whose humour, 'tis time
now, should begin to loath the levity and balladry of
our neighbours : The attempt he confesses to be bold
and daring, there being Pens and Artists of more
eminent abilities, much better qualifi'd for the imploy-
ment than his, or himself, which he well hopes these
his weak endeavours, will in due time provoke, and
enflame to a more accurate undertaking.   He is not
asham'd to own his unskilfulness in Italian Language;

but that's the unhappiness of his Education, which cannot justly be accounted his fault, however he thinks he may warrantably affirm, that he is not mistaken in the power of the Italian Notes, or elegancy of their Compositions, which he would recommend to the English Artists. There has been neither care, nor industry wanting, as well in contriving, as revising the whole Work; which had been abroad in the world much sooner, but that he has now thought fit to cause the whole Thorough Bass to be Engraven, which was a thing quite beside his first Resolutions. It remains only that the English Practitioner be enform'd, that he will find a few terms of Art perhaps unusual to him, the chief of which are these following: *Adagio* and *Grave* which imports nothing but a very slow movement: *Presto, Largo*, and *Vivace*, a very brisk, swift, or fast movement: *Piano*, soft. The Author has no more to add, but his hearty wishes, that his Book may fall into no other hands but theirs who carry Musical Souls about them; for he is willing to flatter himself into a belief, that with Such his labours will seem neither unpleasant, nor unprofitable. Vale."

The foregoing preface is eminently characteristic of the unassuming and retiring disposition of Purcell. The sonatas have never been printed in score, but a few masterly movements selected from the parts and reduced for the pianoforte are inserted in Dr. Crotch's specimens of ancient music; a perusal of these will whet the appetite for more music of such sterling quality.

This year, 1683, was a prolific one with Purcell, for we find that he composed another " Ode, or Welcome Song for the King," commencing, " Fly bold rebellion," and also an ode to celebrate the marriage of George,

Prince of Denmark, with the Princess Anne, afterwards Queen. The marriage took place in July. The words of the ode commence, " From hardy climes." A large manuscript volume entirely in Purcell's hand, is still in existence, which shows that he had been busy from June, 1680, to February, 1683, in composing Fantasias in three, four, five, six, seven, and eight parts; the book in which these are written was evidently the commencement of what was intended to be a complete and lasting record of the composer's works, and perhaps it was intended for presentation to the King.

The publication of the sonatas was soon followed by another entitled, " A musical entertainment perform'd on November xxii. 1683 ; it being the festival of St. Cecilia, a great Patroness of Music, whose Memory is annually honoured by a Public Feast made on that day by the Masters and lovers of Music as well in England as in foreign parts. London : Printed by J. Playford, junior, and are to be sold by John Playford near the Temple Church, and John Carr, at the Middle Temple Gate, 1684."

The book, unlike the sonatas, which were beautifully engraven, is a wretched specimen of type-printing, and copies of it are now very rare. The Preface was addressed,

" To the Gentlemen of the Musical Society, and particularly the Stewards for the year ensuing, William Bridgman, Esq., Nicholas Staggins, Doctor in Music, Gilbert Dolben, Esq., and Mr. Francis Forcer. Gentlemen, your kind Approbation and benign Reception of the performance of these *Musical Compositions* on *St. Cecilia's Day*, by way of Gratitude, claim this Dedication ; which likewise furnishes the Author with an

opportunity of letting the World know the Obligations
he lies under to you; and that he is to all Lovers of
Music, a real Friend and Servant.—HENRY PURCELL."

The music consists of an introductory symphony,
choruses, and soli, with accompaniments for strings, and
has a very novel termination to the words " Iô Cecilia."
The words are poor, and were written by Christopher
Fishbourne,[1] who seems to have been both a poet and
a musician, but of no great pretension in either art.
Purcell's enthusiasm and industry are well exemplified
by the amount of music which he wrote for the first
public observance of St. Cecilia's Day in this country.
In addition to the ode already mentioned as published,
he composed two other odes, one in English and one in
Latin; the former is remarkable for being scored without
any part for the tenor violin, and without parts for
counter-tenor voices, although the latter voice was in
great favour in Purcell's day, and his music generally
abounds with solos for that voice. The Latin ode is
interesting as being scored for three men's voices with
accompaniments for two violins and bass. Both these
odes remain at present in manuscript. The Fitzwilliam
Library at Cambridge possesses a large volume of
manuscript music in the handwriting of Dr. Blow, and
internal evidence shows that it must have been completed in 1683 ; it contains the following anthems by

[1] This we learn from several advertisements of later date,
where it is stated, " At John Carr's shop may be had the musical
entertainment for last St. Cecilia's Day. The words made by Mr.
Christopher Fishburn, and set to music in two, three, four, and
six parts by Mr. Henry Purcell, Composer in Ordinary to His
Sacred Majesty, and one of the Organists of His Majesty's
Chappel Royal."

D

Purcell:—1. " By the Waters of Babylon ;" 2. " O God Thou hast cast us out ;" 3. " Remember not, Lord, our Offences ;" 4. " I will Sing unto the Lord ;" 5. " Blessed be the Lord my Strength ;" 6. " O Lord, our Governour ;" 7. " Let God Arise ;" 8. " Blessed is He ;" 9. " Hear me, O Lord ;" 10. " Bow down Thine Ear ;" 11. " Jerusalem is Built ;" 12. " My Beloved Spake ;" 13. " O God, Thou art my God ;" 14. " Lord, who can tell ?" 15. " Benedicite " in B ♭.

The year 1684 is notable for the remarkable organ competition at the Temple Church, in which the two great organ-builders of the day, Father Smith and Renatus Harris, exhibited their skill by erecting rival organs for the approval of the benchers of the Temple, and which eventually resulted in the selection and retention of the splendid instrument built by Smith. The organ then chosen is still standing in the church and eloquently proclaims the fame of its builder. How far Smith's success was due to the judicious choice he made of organists to show off the qualities and varieties of his stops, it is only possible now to guess, but certainly no more skilful performers could have been found than Dr. Blow and Henry Purcell. Smith's rival, Harris, was also fortunate in obtaining the services of John Baptist Draghi, the friend of Purcell previously mentioned, and whose skill and popularity as an organist contemporary records frequently mention. Smith's organ had the singular advantage of possessing keys for two extra quarter-tones in each octave, which enabled the performer to use distinct pitches or sounds for G sharp and A flat, and also for D sharp and E flat. Those who are familiar with Purcell's sacred music will readily understand what use he would have made of these additional facilities for modulating into remote keys. In his anthems he frequently wrote chords which must have sounded most crude and harsh on all the keyed instruments of his day, tuned as they were on unequal temperament. Purcell, we know, was on very intimate terms with Smith, who was not only an organ-builder, but also an organist,[1] and it is quite probable that it was at Purcell's suggestion that he added the quarter-tones which constituted so remarkable a feature in the Temple organ. In 1684 Purcell composed yet another " Ode, or Welcome Song, on the King's return to Whitehall after his summer's progress ; " the words, commencing, "From these serene and rapturous joys," were written by Thomas Flatman.

In 1685 Purcell was actively concerned in super-intending the erection of an organ in Westminster Abbey expressly for the coronation of James II. and his queen. On April 23rd he was paid the sum of 34*l.* 12*s.* for his services out of the " secret service money." This organ was evidently a small instrument erected just behind the seats occupied by the "King's Choir of Vocal Music," who sat in a gallery in front of and under a south chancel arch, the second from the transept, whilst opposite them, in a similar gallery, were placed the " King's Instrumental Musick." For the coronation service Purcell produced two anthems, " I was Glad," and " My Heart is Inditing," but it would seem that he did not officiate at the organ, for we find that " Purcell, Blow, Child, and Staggins," sang with the basses in the choir on that occasion.

[1] Smith was organist of St. Margaret, Westminster.

In this same year he composed **an** ode in honour of King James, commencing, "Why are all the Muses mute?" and it is very likely that he also composed the music for the tragedy of *Circe* at or about this period. This play, the work of Charles Davenant, when first produced, was accompanied by music from the pen of John Banister,[1] some of which was published in 1679.

A few years since Dr. Rimbault unfortunately published a portion of Purcell's music to *Circe* with Banister's name attached as the composer,[2] but he afterwards discovered the error he had fallen into.[3] *Circe* is one of Purcell's best dramatic works, and contains music which no other composer of his time could have written; it still remains in manuscript. Only music to the first act is now to be found. Perhaps Purcell never completed it.

In 1686 Purcell was again afflicted by the death of a child who had been christened Thomas in remembrance of the deceased uncle. The infant was buried in the cloisters of Westminster Abbey. In this year Purcell composed the music for Dryden's tragedy, *Tyrannic Love,* in which there are several effective and elegant pieces, notably "Hark, my Daridcar," a duet, and "Ah, how sweet it is to love," a song. In addition to this, he wrote another "Ode, or Welcome Song for the King," commencing, "Ye tuneful Muses."

In 1687 Purcell had another son born who was

---

[1] So spelt in the registers of Westminster Abbey, but "Banester" on his monument.

[2] See No. 15 of *The Ancient Vocal Music of England,* by E. F. Rimbault, published by Novello & Co.

[3] See *Concordia,* April 15 and 22, 1876.

named Henry, but he survived only two months, and was buried with his kindred in the cloisters of Westminster Abbey. Purcell composed another " Ode in honour of King James," commencing " Sound the trumpet, beat the drum," in which occurs a duet to the words, " Let Cæsar and Urania live ; " this became so great a favourite that succeeding composers were wont to insert it in their own royal birthday odes. This practice continued till the close of the succeeding century.

About this time Purcell composed a " March " and a " Quickstep," which soon became popular and familiar to the soldiers ; a short time afterward some one, probably Lord Wharton, the Irish Viceroy, with much foresight and wisdom, selected the tune of the " Quickstep" as a vehicle for making known the absurd verses of the song called " Lillibullero." Thanks to the music, the song spread like wildfire, with the result described by Bishop Burnet, who says, " A foolish ballad was made at that time, treating the Papists, and chiefly the Irish, in a very ridiculous manner, which had a burden said to be Irish words, ' Lero, lero, lillibullero,' that made an impression on the army that cannot be imagined by those that saw it not. The whole army, and at last the people, both in city and country, were singing it perpetually, and perhaps never had so slight a thing so great an effect." The Viceroy " boasted that the song had sung a deluded Prince out of the three kingdoms." Other testimony speaks of the song " having contributed not a little towards the great Revolution of 1688."

The earliest existing printed copies of these tunes

are dated 1686, but he reprinted the "Quickstep" in 1689, under the title of "A new Irish tune," in a work called *Musick's Handmaid for the Virginals or Harpsichord;* and he again used the tune as a ground-bass to a piece of incidental music In the play of *The Gordian Knot Unty'd.* The music of "Lillibullero" remains in use to this day in the north of Ireland as a political and party tune, but its use is discontinued by our military bands out of respect for the feelings of our Irish Roman Catholic brethren.

In 1687 Henry Playford published *A Pastoral Elegy on the Death of Mr. John Playford, the Words by Mr. Tate, set to Musick by Mr. Henry Purcell.* It has commonly been believed that this was an elegy on "honest John," as he was familiarly called, but in truth it was in memory of the youngest son of the celebrated old publisher. We have no particulars of his death, but judging from the words of the elegy it must have occurred suddenly :—

> "Then waste no more in sighs your breath,
> Nor think his fate was hard ;
> There's no such thing as sudden death
> To those that always are prepar'd."

This John Playford was only twenty-one years of age when he died; he had commenced business as a music publisher, and would seem to have been remarkable for amiability and piety.

In January, 1688, Purcell, by virtue of his office as "composer in ordinary to his Majesty," received instructions from the King, James II., to compose an anthem to be performed at the Chapel Royal on the 25th of that month, a day which was commanded to be observed as a general thanksgiving in London and twelve miles round, in consequence of the supposed pregnancy of the Queen. As news travelled but slowly in those days, places beyond the radius named were commanded to keep the 29th as a day of joyful thanksgiving. For the occasion Purcell wrote the anthem commencing, "Blessed are they that fear the Lord;" it is scored for the usual solo voices and chorus, with accompaniments for the organ and quartet of strings.

In May, 1688, Purcell had a daughter born, she was baptized in Westminster Abbey, receiving the name of Frances. This child attained to years of maturity, surviving both her father and her mother.

This year was a troublous one; the political horizon was black, and the national fortunes were in great jeopardy, people had small time or inclination for public amusements, but Purcell contributed music for at least one play, *The Fool's Preferment, or the Three Dukes of Dunstable*, a comedy by D'Urfey. The songs were sung by William Mountford, who, Colley Cibber says,[1] " sung a clear counter-tenor, and had a melodious warbling throat." "His voice was clear, full, and melodious."

Mountford was a great favourite with the public as an actor and singer, and he was also a dramatic author, but his career was brought to an untimely end in his thirty-third year by Lord Mohun and Captain Hill, who murdered him in revenge for the part he took in preventing the abduction of the celebrated actress, Mrs. Bracegirdle.

[1] *Apology for the Life of Colley Cibber.*

The songs in the *Fool's Preferment*, were published
with the play soon after its production at the Queen's
Theatre in Dorset Gardens, the title partly reads
" together with all the songs and notes to 'em. Excellently compos'd by Mr. Henry Purcell." Purcell still
continued composing for the church; an anthem, " The
Lord is King," bearing date 1688. He also composed
one more " Ode or Welcome Song" for James II.;
the last music he had occasion to pen for this King.

Curiously we find that Purcell again became *Copyist*
of Westminster Abbey in this year; he succeeded
Charles Taylour, but for what reason has not been
discovered. No information respecting Taylour can
now be found.

In December the unhappy monarch, James II., fled
from his throne and kingdom, and was succeeded by
William and Mary, who were crowned at Westminster
Abbey in 1689, and in connection with that event a
curious story is told by Hawkins :—[1]

" In the beginning of the year 1689 he (Purcell) became
engaged in a dispute with Dr. Sprat, the then Dean, and
the Chapter of Westminster, the occasion whereof was
this. It seems that at the coronation of King William
and Queen Mary, he had received and claimed as his
right, the money taken for admission into the organ
loft of persons desirous of being near spectators of that
ceremony, which for the following reasons must be
supposed to have amounted to a considerable sum ; the
profit arising to the owner of one of the houses at the
west end of the Abbey, where only the procession
could be viewed, amounted at the last coronation to

[1] *History of Music*, Novello's Edition, vol. ii. p. 743.

five hundred pounds. The organ in Purcell's time was on the north side of the choir, and was much nearer the altar than now, so that the spectators from thence might behold the whole of the august ceremony. A sum like that which this must be presumed to have been was worth contending for, and if Purcell had the authority of precedent for his support, he was right in retaining it as a perquisite arising from his office; but his masters thought otherwise, and insisted on it as their due, for in an old Chapter book I find the following entry : ' 18 April, 1689, Mr. Purcell, the organ-blower, to pay to Mr. Needham such money as was received by him for places in the organ-loft, and in default thereof his place to be declared null and void, and that his stipend or salary to be detained in the treasurer's hands until further orders.' Upon which it may be observed that the penning of it is an evidence of great ignorance or malice, in that it describes him by the appellation of organ-blower who was the organist of their own church, and in truth the most excellent musician of his time. What the issue of this contest was does not appear. It may be supposed either that he refunded the money, or compounded the matter with the Dean and Chapter, it being certain that he continued to execute his office for some years after."

The above account in Sir John Hawkins's hand is now lying before me with a note that it is to be inserted in vol. iv. p. 497; it fills two pages of letter paper, and on the third page of the same sheet is a further note by Dr. Benjamin Cooke, which certainly ought to have been printed with the foregoing :—

" The order herein alluded to is not the real entry in the Chapter minutes, but is in another old book which contains copies or memorandums of many of the

Chapter minutes, and probably was the rough draft, or it might be done by Mr. Needham afterwards from his recollection, and so the wording is different tho' the substance of both is the same, and this book was shown to me, and afterwards by my desire to Sir John Hawkins, at which time we understood it to be the original Chapter minutes, but have since been convinced of the contrary by having seen the original minute; and in this last he is not described by the title of *Organ-blower*, as he is in the former, but he is stil'd organist.—B. C."

Whatever may have been the end of this dispute, it probably was speedily concluded, for we find by the Abbey registers of the 6th September following, that Purcell had an infant son baptized in the Abbey, who received the name of Edward; this child survived his parents and became an organist of some note.

On the 5th of August, 1689, a new ode by Purcell, called "A Welcome Song at the Prince of Denmark's Coming Home," and commencing, "Celestial music," was performed at Mr. Maidwell's, a schoolmaster. In commemoration of the accession of William and Mary, Tom D'Urfey prepared an ode abounding in praise of "The Great Nassau." This Purcell set to music, and it was subsequently performed at a cost of £100 in the "Merchant Taylors' Hall," at the gathering of the natives of the County of York at their feast, March 27th, 1690; from which circumstance the ode is known as "The Yorkshire Feast Song." The music became extremely popular; portions of it were printed in the *Orpheus Britannicus*, and other collections, and the entire work was printed by Goodison in 1788 or 1789,

but in a very incorrect fashion. It has lately been
published in a very satisfactory manner by the new
" Purcell Society."

In the year 1690 Purcell must have worked assidu-
ously for the theatres ; we can trace to this period the
production of *The Tempest,* an alteration from Shakespeare by Shadwell ; *The Prophetess,* or *Dioclesian,* an
adaptation from Beaumont and Fletcher by Betterton ;
the *Massacre of Paris,* by Lee ; and *Amphitryon,* by
Dryden.

The music of *The Tempest* is extremely beautiful,
witness " Come unto these Yellow Sands " and " Full
Fathom Five," which are known and admired and in
vogue to this day. These pieces being allied to
Shakespeare's lines are not likely to be superseded by
other composers' music, but unfortunately the major
part of Purcell's work in *The Tempest* is married to
verse not Shakespeare's, and cannot therefore find any
fitting place in a performance of the play.

Dioclesian, at first called *The Prophetess,* was adver-
tised for publication in the *London Gazette,* July 3rd,
1690 :—

" The vocal and instrumental musick in the opera
called *The Prophetess,* composed by Mr. Henry Purcell,
is designed to be printed by way of subscriptions. Proposals may be seen at Mr. John Carr's shop at the
Middle Temple Gate, and at Mr. Henry Playford's shop
near the Inner Temple Church, who are appointed to
take subscriptions."

It was published the following year with the title,
" *The Vocal and Instrumental Musick of the Prophetess,*

or the History of Dioclesian, composed by Henry Purcell, Organist of their Majesties' Chappel, and of St.
Peter's, Westminster.   London, Printed by J. Heptinstall, for the Author, and are to be sold by John Carr,
at his shop at the Middle Temple Gate near Temple-
Barr.   M.DCXCI."

The libretto was made into a so-called opera.   Purcell
dedicated the work to the Duke of Somerset, and, as
was the manner of the times, introduced his published
score of the music with a flowery preface; it contains
many interesting passages and reads as follows :—

"Your Grace has been pleas'd so particularly to
favour the Composition of the Musick in *Dioclesian,*
that from thence I have been encourag'd to this presumption of Dedicating not only It, but also the unworthy
Author of it to your Protection.   All Arts and Sciences
have receiv'd their first encouragement from Great
Persons, and owe their Propagation and Success to
their esteem : like some sort of Fruit-trees, which being
of a tender Constitution, and delicate in their Nature,
require the shadow of the Cedar to shield their Infancy
from Blites and Storms.

"Music and Poetry have ever been acknowledged
Sisters, which walking hand in hand supports each
other; As Poetry is the harmony of Words, So Musick
is that of Notes: and as Poetry is a Rise above Prose
and Oratory, so is Musick the exaltation of Poetry.
Both of them may excel apart, but sure they are most
excellent when they are joyn'd because nothing is then
wanting to either of their Perfections : for thus they
appear like Wit and Beauty in the same Person.
Poetry and Painting have arriv'd to their perfection in
our own Country: Musick is yet but in its Nonage, a
forward Child which gives hope of what it may be

hereafter in ENGLAND, when the Masters of it shall find more Encouragement. 'Tis now learning ITALIAN, which is its best Master, and studying a little of the French Air, to give it somewhat more of Gayety and Fashion. Thus being farther from the Sun, we are of later Growth than our Neighbour Countries, and must be content to shake off our Barbarity by degrees. The present Age seems already dispos'd to be refin'd, and to distinguish betwixt wild Fancy, and a just, numerous Composition. So far the Genius of your Grace has already prevail'd on Us. Many of the Nobility and Gentry have followed your Illustrious Example in the Patronage of Musick. Nay, even our Poets begin to grow asham'd of their harsh and broken Numbers, and promise to file our uncouth Language into smoother Words. Once more, therefore, I presume to offer Myself and this Composition with all humility to Your Grace's Protection, at least till I can redeem so mean a Present by One which may better deserve Your Acceptation. Be pleas'd to pardon my Ambition, which had no other means to obtain the Honour of being made known to You, but only this. The Town, which has been so indulgent to my first Endeavours in this kind, has encourag'd me to proceed in the same Attempt; and Your Favour to this Trifle will be a good Omen not only to the Success of the Next, but also to all the future Performances of Your Grace's most Obedient and most Obliged Servant,

" HENRY PURCELL."

The music of *Dioclesian* is scored for " 1st Violins, 2nd Violins, Tener Violins, Base Violins, 2 Flutes, 3 Hautboys (1st, 2nd, and Tener), 1 Basoon and 2 Trumpets;" the vocal parts have solos for all the voices, and there are numerous choruses. It is evident Purcell regarded this work with some affection and pride; all the printed copies were corrected by his own hand. At the end of the book is printed the following :—

"Advertisement. In order to the speedier Publication of this Book, I employed two several Printers ; but One of them falling into some trouble, and the Volume swelling to a Bulk beyond my expectation, have been the Occasions of this Delay.

"It has been objected that some of the Songs are already common ; but I presume that the Subscribers, upon perusal of the Work, will easily be convinced that they are not the Essential Parts of it. I have, according to my Promise in the Proposals, been very carefull in the Examination of every Sheet, and hope the Whole will appear as Correct as any yet Extant. My desire to make it as cheap as possibly I cou'd to the Subscribers, prevail'd with me so far above the consideration of my own Interest, that I find too late the Subscription money will scarcely amount to the Expense of compleating this Edition."

Although *Dioclesian* did not prove a lucrative investment for the composer it must have added considerably to his fame ; produced at the Queen's Theatre in 1690, Downes, in his *Roscius Anglicanus*, says, "It gratify'd the expectation of Court and City ; and got the author great reputation." One of the airs in the piece, "What shall I do to show how much I love her," was afterwards adapted to the words, "Virgins are like the Fair Flower in its Lustre," and did duty as a part of *The Beggar's Opera*.

The songs from *Amphitryon*[1] were published by Heptinstall soon after the production of the comedy.

[1] "*The Songs in Amphitryon, with the Musick.* Composed by Mr. Henry Purcell. London : printed by J. Heptinstall for Jacob Tonson, at the Judge's Head in Chancery Lane. MDCXC."

Purcell's music for *Dioclesian* and for *Amphitryon* seems to have opened the eyes of Dryden, who had evidently been blind to the distinguished talent of the composer. In the *Epistle Dedicatory* to *Amphitryon*, dated October 24, 1690, Dryden says :—

" What has been wanting on my part has been abundantly supplyed by the Excellent Composition of Mr. *Purcell ;* in whose Person we have at length found an *Englishman* equal with the best abroad. At least my Opinion of him has been such, since his happy and judicious Performances in the late Opera,[1] and the Experiences I have had of him, in the setting of my three Songs for this *Amphitryon :* To all which, and particularly to the Composition of the *Pastoral Dialogue,* the numerous Quire of Fair Ladies gave so just an Applause on the Third Day."

In addition to the before-mentioned plays, Purcell composed in 1690 the music for D'Urfey's " Ode for the Queen's Birthday, April 29," commencing " Arise, my muse," and also an ode for King William beginning with the words, " Sound the trumpet."

We find that he again resigned his appointment as Copyist at Westminster Abbey, and was succeeded by Edward Braddock, who was one of the Lay Vicars and Master of the Choristers, and also a Gentleman of the Chapels Royal.

In the succeeding year, 1691, Purcell produced the music for *King Arthur*, written by Dryden. It was one of Purcell's most elaborate and most successful efforts in dramatic composition, and contains several pieces which have always been held in popular favour.

[1] *Dioclesian.*

The solo and chorus, " Come, if you Dare," is to this day one of the most stirring and effective displays which a tenor vocalist could select, and is therefore frequently heard. The whole of the frost scene is remarkable from its vocal realism of intense and freezing cold. The peculiar and original effects here introduced by Purcell were afterwards copied by Jeremiah Clark, a fellow-student of Purcell, in the anthem, " I will love Thee, O Lord." Mention must also be made of the lovely duet, " Two daughters of this aged stream."

Unfortunately no complete copy of the score of this work, the outcome of the composer's mature judgment, exists. It is presumed that Purcell wrote only one perfect copy, which was retained by the managers of the theatre, who, jealous of possible rivals, would neither permit it to be copied in manuscript or printed.[1] The success at the time of its production is thus recorded by Downes in his *Roscius Anglicanus*:—

"*King Arthur*, an opera, wrote by Mr. Dryden; it was excellently adorned with scenes and machines: the musical part set by the famous Mr. Henry Purcell, and Dances made by Mr. Jo. Priest: the play and musick pleas'd the Court and City, and being well perform'd 'twas very gainful to the company."

Dryden's courtly servility has been deplored by more than one author. He had followed the lead set by Charles II., who had imported Monsieur Grabu from France, and set him up as a musical king, and for him, by royal command, Dryden wrote the opera of

[1] North, in the *Memoires of Musick*, 1728, mentions Purcell's *King Arthur* as at that time " unhappily lost."

Albion and Albanius. In the preface to the work he says :—

" The best judges, and those too of the best quality, who have honoured his (Grabu's) rehearsals with their presence, have no less commended the happiness of his genius than his skill. These and other qualities have raised M. Grabu to a degree above any man who shall pretend to be his rival on our stage."

The composer who was thus set above Purcell appears to have enjoyed a somewhat exalted opinion of his own ability, as will be seen by the following extract from the dedication of *Albion and Albanius*, addressed to James II. by Grabu himself :—

" As the subject of this opera is naturally magnificent, it could not but excite my genius, and raise it to a greater height in the composition—even so as to surpass itself. The only displeasure which remains with me is, that I could not possibly be furnished with variety of excellent voices to present it to your Majesty in full perfection."

Contrast this bumptious self-assertion with the modest prefaces of Purcell previously quoted. However, notwithstanding the patronage of the King and the flatteries of Dryden, *Albion and Albanius* proved a great failure : it was performed only six times, and from the date of its last performance (1685) Dryden became impressed with the conviction that he must look elsewhere for his future composer, and, as we have already seen, he at last recognised the merits of Purcell. In the preface to *King Arthur*, intended by Dryden as a sequel to *Albion and Albanius*, the author says, " he submitted

E

himself in writing and preparing it for the stage "
entirely to the guidance of Purcell. This confession
was probably made with considerable compunction.

The following extracts from Dryden's *Epistle Dedicatory*, prefixed to the libretto, will be read with interest :—

" I humbly offer you this trifle, which if it succeed
upon the stage, is like to be the chiefest Entertainment
of our Ladies and Gentlemen this summer.   When I
wrote it, seven years ago, I employ'd some reading
about it, to inform myself out of Beda, Bochartus, and
other authors, concerning the rites and customs of the
heathen Saxons; as I also used the little skill I have
in Poetry to adorn it.   But not to offend the present
times, nor a government which has hitherto protected
me, I have been obliged so much to alter the first
design, and take away so many beauties from the
writing, that it is now no more what it was formerly,
than the ship of the *Royal Sovereign*, after so often
taking down, and altering, to the vessel it was at the first
building. There is nothing better, than what I intended,
than the Musick ; which has since arriv'd to a greater
perfection in England, than ever formerly; especially
passing through the artful hands of Mr. *Purcel*, who
has compos'd it with so great a genius, that he has
nothing to fear but an ignorant, ill-judging audience.
But the numbers of poetry and vocal musick, are sometimes so contrary, that in many places I have been
oblig'd to cramp my Verses, and make them rugged to
the reader, that they may be harmonious to the hearer :
of which I have no reason to repent me, because these
sorts of Entertainments are principally design'd for the
ear and the eye ; and therefore, in reason, my art on
this occasion ought to be subservient to his."

Dryden had evidently by this time become aware

of Purcell's superiority to his contemporary musical
brethren; the poet and musician met on intimate and
friendly terms. It is recorded that Purcell, by virtue
of his court appointments, had an apartment in the clock
tower of St. James's Palace, and that Dryden when in
debt availed himself of his friendship with Purcell, to
escape arrest by taking refuge in Purcell's room, where
he was perfectly safe, and could moreover enjoy the air
and exercise in the Palace gardens.[1]

King Arthur after many years of neglect, possibly in
consequence of the loss of the score of the music, was
revived at Drury Lane theatre in 1770 with enormous
success; again in 1781, in 1784, in 1803, and in 1842.
The music remained unpublished until 1843, when it was
edited by Edward Taylor, the Gresham music professor,
and printed by the " Musical Antiquarian Society."
Unfortunately the edition is imperfect, several pieces
being still wanting, and of those which are printed we
can be quite certain that they are not presented to us
in the complete form composed by Purcell: for instance,
the first overture is simply scored for strings, whereas
Purcell freely uses flutes, hautboys, and trumpets in
other parts of the work. Professor Taylor could find
no trace of this overture excepting in the *Theatre Ayres*
published by Mrs. Purcell in 1697, a collection which
only gave string parts. Whilst speaking of Dryden and
Purcell it will be well to correct a great blunder made
by Hawkins in his *History of Music ;* he writes:—

"It is said that Dryden wrote his *Alexander's Feast*
with a view to its being set by Purcell, but that Purcell

[1] *Round about Piccadilly*, by Wheatley, p. 294.

declined the task, as thinking it beyond the power of
music to express sentiments so superlatively energetic
as that ode abounds with ; the truth of the assertion may
well be questioned, seeing that he composed the *Te
Deum*, and scrupled not to set to music some of the
most sublime passages in the Psalms, the Prophecy of
Isaiah, and other parts of Holy Scriptures." [1]

Had Hawkins made proper inquiry he would have
discovered that *Alexander's Feast* was not written by
Dryden until two years after Purcell's death.   This
fact is verified by a letter addressed by Dryden to his
son in September, 1697, in which he says : " I am
writing a song for *St. Cecilia's Feast*," and by the
additional testimony of Mr. St. John, afterwards Lord
Bolingbroke.[2]

In 1691 Purcell composed the music for *Distressed
Innocence*, a tragedy by Elkanah Settle, and also for the
comedies called the *Gordian Knot Untyed*, by an anony-
mous author, and *Sir Anthony Love* by Southerne.   In
addition to these works he wrote an "Ode for the Queen's
Birthday," commencing " Welcome glorious morn."

In 1692, he composed music for the plays, entitled,
the *Wife's Excuse*, by Southerne ; the *Indian Queen*, by
Howard and Dryden ; the *Indian Emperour*, by Dryden ;
Œdipus, a tragedy by Dryden and Lee ; the *Marriage-
hater match'd*, by D'Urfey ; and the so-called opera,
the *Fairy Queen*, anonymously adapted from Shakespeare's *Midsummer Night's Dream*.   The music of the
Indian Queen abounds in very striking passages ; it is

[1] Hawkins's *History of Music*, vol. ii. p. 753.
[2] See Sir Walter Scott's *Life of Dryden*.

only necessary to recall the titles of "Ye Twice ten
Hundred Deities," which Dr. Burney considered the
best recitative in the English language; the dramatic
air, " By the Croaking of the Toad," and the delightful
song, " I Attempt from Love's Sickness to fly," a ditty
again made popular by the exquisite singing of Hobbs
in the generation just passed away.[1]

Three years after the first performance of the *Indian
Queen*, some portion of the music was published without the consent, or even consultation, of the composer;
the publication, now become very rare, has the following
title :—

" The songs in the *Indian Queen*, as it is now compos'd into an opera by Mr. Henry Purcell, composer
in ordinary to his Majesty, and one of the organists
of his Majesty's Chapel Royal. London. Printed by
J. Heptinstall, and are now to be sold by John May,
at his shop under St. Dunstan's church ; and for
John Hudgbutt at Thomas Dring's, bookseller at the
Harrow at Clifford's-lane-end in Fleet Street, 1695."

The preface is too curious to be omitted : —

" The publishers to Mr. Henry Purcell. Sir, having
had the good Fortune to meet with the Score or Original
Draught of your Incomparable Essay of Musick
compos'd for the Play, call'd the *Indian Queen*, It
soon appear'd that we had found a Jewel of very
great Value ; on which account we were unwilling
that so rich a Treasure should any longer lie bury'd
in Oblivion ; and that the Commonwealth of Musick
should be depriv'd of so considerable a Benefit. Indeed,
we well knew your innate Modesty to be such, as not
to be easily prevailed upon to set forth anything in

[1] Hogarth's *Memoirs of the Musical Drama*, 1838.

Print, much less to Patronize your own Works,
although in some respects Inimitable. But in regard
that (the Press being now open) any one might print
an imperfect Copy of these admirable Songs, or publish
them in the nature of a Common Ballad, We were so
much the more emboldened to make this Attempt, even
without acquainting you with our Design ; not doubting
but your accustomed Candor and Generosity will induce
you to pardon this Presumption. As for our parts,
if you shall think fit to condescend so far, we shall
always endeavour to approve ourselves your obedient
servants,   " J. May,
                                   " J. Hudgebutt."

Comment on this legal robbery of the fruit of an
author's brain-work is quite unnecessary.

The music to *Œdipus* is very dramatic, but not of
great importance. That of the *Fairy Queen*, on the
contrary, is of considerable pretension and was a great
success. Downes, in his *Roscius Anglicanus*, says :—

"This in ornaments was superior to the other two (*King
Arthur* and *Dioclesian*), especially in cloaths for all the
singers and dancers ; scenes, machines, and decorations,
all most profusely set off, and excellently perform'd :
chiefly the instrumental and vocal part compos'd by
the said Mr. Purcell, and dances by Mr. Priest. The
Court and town were wonderfully satisfy'd with it, but
the expences in setting it out being so great the company
got little by it."

A portion of the music was published by the composer with the title, "Some select songs as they are
sung in the *Fairy Queen*, set to musick by Mr. Henry
Purcell, London. Printed by J. Heptinstall for the

Author, and are to be sold by John Carr, at the Inner
Temple Gate, near Temple Barr, by Henry Playford
at his shop in the Temple, and at the Theatre in Dorset
Gardens, 1692."

A few pieces from the opera were also published
separately; one beginning " Now the maids and the
men," with the curious heading " A Dialogue in the
Opera call'd the *Fairy Queen,* set by Mr. Henry Purcell,
sung by Mr. Reading[1] and Mr. Pate (in Woman's
habit), and exactly engrav'd by Tho. Cross."

The Fairy Queen seems to have shared the fate of
much other music of Purcell's, for the *London Gazette,*
Oct. 13th, 1700, has the following advertisement :—
" The score of the musick for the *Fairy Queen* set by
the late Mr. Henry Purcell, and belonging to the
Patentees of the Theatre Royal in Covent Garden,
London, being lost by his death, whosoever brings
the said score, or a copy thereof, to Mr. Zackary Baggs,
Treasurer of the said Theatre, shall have 20 guineas
reward." The advertisement was repeated, evidently
without any successful result, as the opera was not
reproduced, but long years afterwards one of the songs,

---

[1] Reading and Pate some three years afterwards figured in
another kind of Duo ; the *Post-Boy,* June 20th, 1695, has the
following paragraph :—" I am informed that the Lord Chamberlain hath been pleased to displace Mr. Pate and Mr. Reading
from their places in the Playhouse for being in the late riot at
Drury Lane." The riot had occurred at the "Dog Tavern," and
in consequence several persons were prosecuted and found guilty;
some were fined 500 marks each, but Reading and Pate were
fined only twenty marks each ; probably their fines were reduced
in consideration of their dismissal by the Lord Chamberlain.
They were, however, soon afterwards reinstated in their previous
appointments.

"If Love's a Sweet Passion," was adapted to words by Gay for the *Beggar's Opera*.

In this same year, 1692, Purcell composed an ode for the Queen's birthday to words of Sir Charles Sedley, commencing "Love's Goddess sure was blind." This ode is notable as containing the song, "May her blest example chase," the bass of which is the melody of the old ballad "Cold and raw," a very popular song of the day. It had been wrought into a catch by John Hilton in 1652, but the reason for its incorporation by Purcell in the Queen's birthday ode is narrated by Hawkins as follows :—

"This tune was greatly admired by Queen Mary, the consort of King William; and she once affronted Purcell by requesting to have it sung to her, he being present. The story is as follows: the Queen having a mind one afternoon to be entertained with music, sent to Mr. Gostling, then one of the chapel, and afterwards sub-dean of St. Paul's, to Henry Purcell and Mrs. Arabella Hunt, who had a very fine voice and an admirable hand on the lute, with a request to attend her; they obeyed her commands; Mr. Gostling and Mrs. Hunt sang several compositions of Purcell, who accompanied them on the harpsichord : at length the Queen beginning to grow tired, asked Mrs. Hunt if she could not sing the old Scots' ballad, 'Cold and raw.' Mrs. Hunt answered yes, and sang it to her lute. Purcell was all the while sitting at the harpsichord unemployed, and not a little nettled at the Queen's preference of a vulgar ballad to his music ; but seeing her majesty delighted with this tune, he determined that she should hear it upon another occasion : and accordingly in the next birthday song, viz. that for the year 1692, he composed an air to the words, 'May her bright example,' the bass whereof is the tune to ' Cold and raw : ' it is printed in the second part of the *Orpheus Britannicus,* and is note for note the same with the Scots' tune."

Hawkins no doubt had this story from Gostling, the son of the Gostling mentioned in the anecdote, and it is therefore probably true.

In the same year he composed one of his most celebrated odes, for the festival held in honour of St. Cecilia at the Stationers' Hall, November 22nd. The *Gentleman's Journal or Monthly Miscellany,* a periodical published immediately afterward, gives an account of the performance as follows :—

" In my first journal I gave you a large account of the music feast on St. Cecilia's Day ; so to avoid repetition, I shall only tell you that the last was in no ways inferior to the former. The following Ode was admirably set to music by Mr. Henry Purcell, and performed twice with universal applause, particularly the second stanza, which was sung with incredible graces by Mr. Purcell himself. Though I was enjoined not to name the author of the Ode, I find a great deal of reluctance to forbear letting you know whom you must thank for so beautiful a poem ; and to use Ovid's words, ' Sequoque nunc, quam vis est quiscere, Quinte Nominet invitum, vix mea, Musa tenet.' "

The author was the Rev. Nicholas Brady of the churches of St. Catherine Cree, and St. Michael, Wood Street, better known as the co-labourer with Tate in the versions of the Psalms published under their joint names.

The *Gentleman's Journal,* January, 1693, has an Epigram " by Mr. B—y, whose Ode for St. Cecilia's

Day you liked so well." The words of the ode were printed in 1782 [1] with Dr. Brady's name as author.

The air which Purcell " sang with incredible graces" we are able to identify by means of various separate publications of the song. The title of one copy printed in 1692 or 1693 reads thus, " Tis Nature's Voice (Ode for St. Cecilia's day), a song set by Mr. H. Purcell, and sung by himself at St. Cecilia's Feast in 1692, the words by N. Brady."

The " incredible graces" are, of course, numerous division passages, commonly called runs. These graces were much in vogue in Purcell's day, and unfortunately he too often pandered to the vulgar taste of the multitude, and injured his music by writing many such, both in his sacred and secular works. The fashion was probably borrowed from the Italians. Bedford, in his *Abuse of Musick*, printed in 1711, says :—

" Among the varieties which have been brought into our musick, the *divisions* of many and short notes to a syllable is the most obvious to every hearer. These must be allowed to be some of the finest *graces* to our modern performances. They are design'd to strike upon the passions, and increase our rapture, and when they are well compos'd and well perform'd they set off the voice in a most excellent and extraordinary manner."

The following curious anecdote told by Tony Aston, in his *Brief Supplement to Colley Cibber*, further illustrates the custom of *gracing* music which descended to our own times :—

[1] *Nichol's Select Collection of Poems.*

" As Mr. Verbruggen had nature for his directress in acting, so had a known singer, Jemmy Bowen, the same in music. He, when practising a song set by Mr. Purcell, some of the musick told him to grace and run a division in such a place. 'O let him alone,' said Mr. Purcel ; 'he will grace it more naturally than you or I can teach him.'"

The "Cecilia Ode" of 1692 was frequently performed, and must have been an especial favourite, if we may judge by the numerous manuscript copies of the score still in existence. The work was published by "The Musical Antiquarian Society" a few years since.

In 1693 Purcell composed music for the plays, the *Old Bachelor*, a comedy by Congreve ; the *Richmond Heiress*, a comedy by D'Urfey ; the *Maid's Last Prayer*, a comedy by Southerne ; and *Henry II.*, a tragedy by Bancroft. In addition to these pieces he composed music for the "Queen's Birthday Ode," commencing "Celebrate this festival," the libretto of which was written by Nahum Tate. The overture to this ode is the same as that to the "Cecilia Ode" of the same year, transposed one note lower, from D to C. It has been printed in a very incorrect manner by Goodison.

One other ode belongs also to this year. It was written by Tate for the commemoration of the centenary of the foundation of Trinity College, Dublin, and commences "Great Parent, hail." It is supposed that the ode was performed at Christ Church, Dublin, on the 9th of January, 1694 ; but no information on the subject has as yet been discovered either at Trinity College or

Christ Church.   The ode was included in Goodison's
"Purcell publications."

In 1694 Purcell revised the twelfth edition of *John
Playford's Introduction to the Skill of Musick*. The third
part of the work, which treats of *The Art of Descant*,[1]
appears to have been almost wholly re-written by
Purcell.   The directions for the use of "discords" were
quite novel for the time, and so also must have been
the paragraph where he says, "Formerly they used to
compose from the *Bass*, but modern authors compose to
the *Treble* when they make *Counterpoint* or *Basses* to
tunes or songs."   Again, in speaking of composition in
three parts, he writes, "The first thing to treat of is
Counterpoint, and in this I must differ from Mr. *Simp-
son* (whose *Compendium* I admire as the most ingenious
book I e're met with on this subject); but his rule in
three parts for *Counterpoint* is too strict and destructive
to good air, which ought to be preferred above such nice
rules." He then goes on to explain that in vocal music
the parts should move smoothly, but that in instrumental music greater freedom would be admissible,
and he points out the Italian composers as worthy
models.   He also gives a "Canon, four in one," by
Dr. Blow, of whom he says, his "character is suffi-
ciently known by his works, of which this very instance
is enough to recommend him for one of the greatest
masters in the world."

---

[1] In the thirteenth edition published in 1697, the third part has
the following heading :—"The art of Descant, or composing
musick in parts ; made very plain and easie by the late Mr.
Henry Purcell."

To Purcell's labours of this year, 1694, we are indebted for the music to the plays of *Don Quixote*, Parts I. and II. Purcell only composed a portion of the music required, but amongst the number are two worthy of particular mention,—a duet, "Sing all ye Muses," and a bass song, "Let the dreadful engines." The libretto was the work of D'Urfey.

Purcell also wrote music for a comedy called the *Married Beau*, by Crowne; for the *Double Dealer*, a comedy by Congreve; for the *Fatal Marriage*, a tragedy by Southerne; and also for *Love Triumphant*,[1] a tragi-comedy by Dryden.

To these must be added another "Ode for the Queen's Birthday," beginning, " Come ye sons of art; " and last and best of all, the great "Te Deum and Jubilate" in D, composed with orchestral accompaniments, the first example of such a work this country had seen.

Composed expressly for the festival of St. Cecilia's Day, 1694, the music was published by Purcell's widow in 1697, with the following dedication :—

" To the Right Reverend Father in God, Nathaniel, Lord Bishop of Durham. My Lord, the ambition I have to do the greatest honour I can to the memory of my Dear Husband, by inscribing some of his best compositions to the best Patrons both of the science he profess'd, and of his performances in it, is the fairest Apology I can make to your Lordship; as it was the main Inducement to myself for placing your Lordship's Name before this Piece of Musick. The Pains he bestow'd in preparing it for so Great and Judicious an Auditory, were highly rewarded by their kind Reception

---

[1] The last piece Dryden wrote for the stage.

of it when it was first Perform'd, and more yet by their
Intention to have it repeated at their *Annual Meeting;*
but will receive the last and highest Honour by your
Lordship's favourable Reception of it from the Press,
to which I have committed it, that I might at once
gratifie the Desires of several gentlemen to see the
Score, and at the same time give myself an opportunity
to acknowledge, in the most Publick and Gratefull
Manner, the many Favours Your Lordship has bestow'd
on my Deceased Husband, and consequently on

> " Your Lordship's
> " Most oblig'd and most Humble Servant,
>   " F. PURCELL."

The intention of annually performing the " Te Deum
and Jubilate " must have been formed in 1697, the year
of publication, as we know that in 1696 Dr. Blow
composed a " Te Deum and Jubilate" which were
performed.   Purcell's work was immediately adopted
by the " Corporation of the Sons of the Clergy " [1] for
performance at their Annual Festival, and its use
continued until Handel, in 1713, composed his "Te
Deum and Jubilate " for the Peace of Utrecht.   After
that time the works of Purcell and Handel were
performed alternately until 1743, when Handel's new
work composed for the victory at Dettingen displaced
the two former compositions.   Of course Handel
must have often heard Purcell's " Te Deum ; " and

---

[1] The music was published by Walsh with the following new
title, " Te Deum et Jubilate for voices and instruments perform'd
before the *Sons of the Clergy* at the Cathedral Church of St. Paul.
Composed by the late Mr. Henry Purcel." This led to a notion
that the music had been composed for the " Sons of the Clergy "
festival.

that he greatly profited by it is evident from the striking resemblance of many passages in his own *Te Deum*, when compared with that of his illustrious predecessor.

But it must in candour be admitted that the remarkable likeness between Purcell's "Te Deum," as it is now performed, and Handel's "Dettingen Te Deum," is greatly due to Dr. Boyce, who, being a thorough Handelian scholar, re-scored and re-arranged Purcell's work.

Queen Mary died on the 28th of December, 1694, and Purcell composed the music for her funeral, which took place the 5th of March following (1695), in Westminster Abbey. Purcell composed two anthems, to the words, "Blessed is the man that feareth the Lord," and "Thou knowest, Lord, the secrets of our hearts." Contemporary records speak in affecting terms of the solemnity of the occasion ;—"the day was dark and troubled, and a few ghastly plumes of snow fell on the black plumes of the funeral car." The procession was attended by the two Houses of Parliament with their maces, "the Lords robed in scarlet and ermine, and the Commons in long black mantles ;" the banners of England and France, Scotland and Ireland, were borne before the corpse. On the gorgeous coffin of purple and gold were laid the crown and sceptre of the realm. Inside the Abbey, the whole of the church, nave, choir, and transepts were all ablaze with innumerable waxlights ; and a little robin-redbreast, who had found refuge from the inclement weather, constantly flew down and perched on the hearse, seeming to the spectators as if he, too, mourned for the Queen who had been so loved and was now so lamented. Of Purcell's music, Dr. Tudway, one of the choir on this occasion, says : " The anthem, ' Blessed is the man,' was composed after the old way, and was sung at the interment of Queen Mary in Westminster Abbey ; a great Queen, and extremely lamented, being there to be interred, everybody present was disposed and serious at so solemn a service, as indeed they ought to be at all parts of Divine worship. I appeal to all that were present, as well such as understood music, as those that did not, whether they ever heard anything so rapturously fine, and solemn, and so heavenly in the operation, which drew tears from all ; and yet a plain natural composition, which shows the power of music, when 'tis rightly fitted and adapted to devotional purposes." The second anthem, " Thou knowest, Lord, the secrets of our hearts," Dr. Tudway says, " was accompanied by flat, mournful trumpets." This majestic movement is a splendid monument to the memory of Purcell. It has been used at every choral funeral in Westminster Abbey and St. Paul's Cathedral since its first production. Dr. Croft, who subsequently set the " Burial Office " to music, refrained from composing to these words, on the ground that the music of Purcell was unapproachable, and adds, that in composing his own music he had endeavoured, as near as possible, to " imitate that great master and celebrated composer, whose name will for ever stand high in the rank of those who have laboured to improve the English style, in his so happily adapting his compositions to English words

in that elegant and judicious manner, as was unknown
to many of his predecessors."

Queen Mary died of small-pox, and the memory of
her goodness was felt so universally by the people that
writers vied with each other in their endeavours to per-
petuate records of her worth. I have now before me a
volume containing thirty-six odes and monodies to her
memory, all published in 1695. Amongst them are an
" Epicedium," set to music by Dr. Blow, the words by
Mr. Herbert; a Latin version of the same, commencing,
" Incassum Lesbia," set to music by Henry Purcell, for
a solo voice; and another beginning, "O dive custos
auriacæ domus," also set to music by Purcell, for two
voices.

Purcell was in a delicate state of health at the time
of writing the music for Queen Mary's funeral, yet he
seems to have worked with undiminished determination,
composing music for the comedy, the *Canterbury Guest*,
written by Ravenscroft; the *Mock Marriage*, a comedy
by Scott; the *Rival Sisters*, a tragedy by Gould;
Oroonoko, a tragedy by Southerne; the *Knight of Malta*,
a play by Beaumont and Fletcher; and *Bonduca, or
the British Heroine*, a tragedy adapted from Beaumont
and Fletcher,—this play included the catch, "Jack,
Thou'rt a Toper," the admirable duets, "To Arms," and
" Britons Strike Home." Some of the music was
printed on single sheets immediately after performance,
but it remained for the " Musical Antiquarian Society "
to issue in 1842 a complete copy of the score, edited by
Dr. Rimbault.

Purcell also, on 24th July in this year, produced

F

a "Birthday Ode" for the Duke of Gloucester. The ode commences, "Who can from joy refrain." It was written for solo voices and chorus with orchestral accompaniments. Among the principal singers at the first performance were Mr. Howell, Mr. Robert, and Mr. Damascene.

Purcell also wrote some music for D'Urfey's third part of *Don Quixote*. Amongst the pieces he contributed to this play was the celebrated cantata, "From Rosie Bowers." This song was frequently reprinted, and with the note that it was "The last song the Author sett, it being in his sickness." It is probable that D'Urfey had hoped to have had the advantage of Purcell's musical skill for the setting of all his verses in the third part of *Don Quixote,* but it would seem that Purcell was too ill to accomplish the work.

"From Rosie Bowers" was considered so important by D'Urfey that he published the music of the third part of *Don Quixote* with the following title :—

"New Songs in the Third Part of the Comical History of *Don Quixote.* Written by Mr. D'Urfey, and sung at the Theatre Royal. With other new songs by Mr. D'Urfey. Being the last piece set to musick by the late Famous Mr. Henry Purcell, Mr. Courtivill, Mr. Akroy'd, and other eminent Masters of the Age. Engrav'd on Copper-Plates. London, printed for Samuel Briscoe, at the Corner-shop of Charles-street, in Russell-street, Covent Garden, 1696. Price Three Shillings. Where are also to be had, the First and Second Parts of Mr. D'Urfey's Songs, set to musick by Mr. Henry Purcell." [1]

[1] This third part is so scarce that probably only one or two perfect copies now exist.

In the year of the publication just named another song was printed, commencing, "Lovely Albina," with the heading, "The last Song that Mr. Henry Purcell sett before he dy'd." But a later edition says, "The last song the author sett before his sickness." There cannot be much doubt, therefore, that the air "From Rosie Bowers" was really Purcell's last work. D'Urfey's print and tradition agree in this.

And now we come to the last scene of all. It is the 21st of November, 1695,—by a curious coincidence the eve of the festival of St. Cecilia, a day so frequently celebrated by Purcell. In a house on the West side of Dean's Yard, Westminster, in a darkened chamber, the dying musician is lying on his couch in full possession of all his faculties, as he himself had just said in his will, but with a thorough knowledge that he was about to pass into the land of shadows. He could possibly hear some faint murmurs of the evensong service wafted from the old Abbey close by, perhaps some well-remembered phrase of one of his own soul-stirring anthems. The psalm of the day which would be chanted at that evening service concluded with words which he had set to music the world was not likely soon to forget—music which still remains unsurpassed in truthfulness and dignity. A more noble or a more fitting death-chant for a child of song it would be difficult to find :—

> "Blessed be the Lord God of Israel,
> From everlasting, and world without end.
> And let all the people say, Amen."

By his bed-side were gathered his aged mother, his

young wife, and his three infant children; and so amid
their sighs and tears his gentle spirit passed into the
better world, there to continue his service of song and
praise in fulness and perfection.

That Purcell was sincerely loved and mourned by
relations and friends we know, and the following
testimony of tender regard will be read with interest.
It is written on the fly-leaf of a copy of his opera
Dioclesian:—[1]

Ex Dono Carissimi Desideratissimique Autoris HENRICI PUR-
CELL Musarum Sacerdotis: Qui Anno Domini 1695 Pridie Festi
S^{tae} Cœcilæ Multis Flebilis occidit, Nulli Flebilior quàm Amico
suo atque Admiratori JACOBO TALBOT.

Translated thus:

The gift of the most beloved and most distinguished author,
HENRY PURCELL, Priest of the Muses, who in the year of our
Lord 1695, the day before the feast of St. Cecilia, died with many
tears, to none more tearfully than to his friend and admirer,
JACOB TALBOT.

Jacob Talbot was a Fellow of Trinity College, Cambridge, and the author of the words of an " Ode for
the Consert at York Buildings, upon the death of
Mr. Purcell," which will be found in the *Orpheus
Britannicus*, 1698.

Purcell was buried on the 26th of November in
Westminster Abbey, beneath the organ which had so
often responded to his skilful touch. The anthems he
had composed for Queen Mary's funeral only a few
months before were again performed, so that Purcell

[1] In my own library.

had rehearsed and inaugurated his own dirge. Doubtless the remembrance of this would bring home to the mourners the intense pathos of the music with double force.

On the grave-stone the following lines were inscribed :

Plaudite, felices superi, tanto hospite ; nostris
Præfuerat, vestris additur ille choris :
Invida nec vobis Purcellum terra reposcat,
Questa decus sedi deliciasque breves.
Tam cito decessisse, modos cui singula debet
Musa, prophana suos, religiosa suos,
Vivit, Io et vivat, dum vicina organa spirant,
Dumque colet numeris turba canora Deum.

Translated thus :

Applaud so great a guest, celestial pow'rs,
Who now resides with you, but once was ours ;
Yet let invidious earth no more reclaim
Her short-lived fav'rite and her chiefest fame ;
Complaining that so permaturely died
Good-nature's pleasure and devotion's pride.
Died ? no, he lives, while yonder organs sound
And sacred echoes to the choir rebound.

Even in 1722 the inscription had become almost illegible from the wear of passing feet, and soon was entirely obliterated. The grave-stone remained in this condition until 1876, when, by the exertions of Mr. Henry F. Turle, son of the respected organist of the Abbey, a private subscription was made which provided funds for placing another stone and restoring the inscription. By permission of the Dean, the following lines were added :—

FRANCISCA
HENRICI PURCELL Uxor,
Cum conjuge sepulta est.
XIV. Feb. MDCCVI.

On the pillar adjacent to the grave there is a tablet with the inscription :—

Here lies Henry Purcell, Esq., who left this life, and is gone to that blessed place where only his harmony can be exceeded. Obiit 21 mo die Novembris, anno ætates suæ 37mo. Annoq. Domini 1695.

This memorial was erected by the Lady Elizabeth Howard, whom Hawkins, and others, have supposed to have been the wife of Dryden, and a pupil of Purcell. Hawkins also inferred that it was Dryden who wrote the inscription for the memorial, and further, that the dedication of the *Orpheus Britannicus* to Lady Elizabeth Howard was intended for Dryden's wife.

All these surmises are wrong. Dryden married Lady Elizabeth Howard, the eldest daughter of the Earl of Berkshire, in 1665, when Purcell was seven years old. Of course, after the marriage the wife ceased to be Lady Elizabeth *Howard* : moreover, her husband's (Dryden) means would scarcely have permitted the serious cost of Purcell's memorial tablet. This was in reality erected by the wife of Sir Robert Howard, the dramatist, who had been associated with Purcell in theatrical composition, and the lady had been a pupil of Purcell; the probability is, therefore, that Sir Robert wrote the inscription.

Purcell made his will on the day of his death; it is important, and reads as follows :—

" In the name of God, Amen. I, Henry Purcell, of the Citty of Westminster, gent., being dangerously ill as to the constitution of my body, but in good and perfect mind and memory (thanks be to God), doe by these presents publish and declare this to be my last Will and Testament. And I doe hereby give and bequeath unto my loveing Wife, Frances Purcell, all my Estate both reall and personall of what nature and kind soever, to her and to her assigns for ever. And I doe hereby constitute and appoint my said loveing Wife my sole Executrix of this my last Will and Testament, revokeing all former Will or Wills. Witnesse my hand and seale this twentieth first day of November, Annoq. Dni., One thousand six hundred ninety-five, and in the seventh yeare of the Raigne of King William the Third, &c. " H. PURCELL.

" Signed, sealed, published, and declared by the said Henry Purcell in the presence of Wm. Ecles, John Capelin. " B. Peters."

Purcell's widow was thus left sole executrix, and she with her children—Frances, aged 7, Edward, aged 6, and Mary Peters, aged 2 years—continued to reside for a time at the house in Great Dean's Yard, from whence, in 1696, Mrs. Purcell issued *A Choice Collection of Lessons for the Harpsichord or Spinnet, composed by the late Mr. Henry Purcell, Organist of his Majesties Chappel Royal, and of St. Peter's, Westminster.* Of this popular little work three editions were speedily exhausted. In 1697 Mrs. Purcell published a collection of *Ten Sonatas in four parts, composed by the late Mr. Henry Purcell,* and also *A Collection of Ayres, compos'd for the Theatre, and upon other occasions, by the late Mr. Henry Purcell;* and in 1698 a further publication of the first volume of *Orpheus Britannicus: A Collection of all the Choicest Songs for one, two, and three voices, compos'd by Mr. Henry Purcell; together with such Symphonies for Violins or Flutes as were by him design'd for any of them : and a thorough-bass to each song ; figur'd for the Organ, Harpsichord, or Theorbolute. All which are placed in their several Keys according to the order of the Gamut.*

To each of the above-mentioned works Mrs. Purcell prefixed dedicatory epistles, and in all of them she speaks in most affectionate terms of her deceased husband; nevertheless, the breath of slander in later years attributed to her some measure of responsibility for her husband's untimely death. Mrs. Purcell eventually removed from the house in Westminster to Richmond, in Surrey, where she died in February, 1706, and was buried on the 14th of that month with her deceased husband in Westminster Abbey, having survived him eleven years. On the 7th of February, 1706, she made a nuncupative will as she sat in the parlour of her dwelling-house, by which she appointed Mr. Thomas Tovey her executor until her daughter, Frances Purcell, should reach the age of eighteen, when she was to be her executrix. Mrs. Purcell goes on to say that, "According to her husband's desire, she had given her deare son (Edward) a good education, and she alsoe did give him all the Bookes of Musicke in generall, the Organ, the double spinett, the single spinett, a silver tankard, a silver watch, two pair of gold buttons, a hair ring, a mourning ring of Dr. Busby's, a Larum clock, Mr. Edward Purcell's picture, handsome furniture for a room, and he was to be maintained until provided for. All the residue of her property she gave to her said daughter Frances." [1]

[1] It is evident from this will that Purcell's youngest child, Mary Peters, had died since her father's decease.

Sir John Hawkins, in his *History of Music*, would seem to suggest that Purcell left his family in distressed circumstances, but the will of the widow, of which he evidently knew nothing, gives a satisfactory refutation of such a surmise. Hawkins also charges Purcell with associating with tavern company; his words are :—

"Mirth and good humour seemed to have been habitual to him; and this is perhaps the best excuse that can be made for those connections and intimacies with Brown and others, which show him not to have been very nice in the choice of his company. Brown spent his life in taverns and ale-houses; the Hole in the Wall in Baldwin's Gardens was the citadel in which he baffled the assaults of creditors and bailiffs, at the same time that he attracted thither such as thought his wit atoned for his profligacy. Purcell seems to have been of that number, and to merit censure for having prostituted his invention, by adapting music to some of the most wretched ribaldry that was ever obtruded on the world for humour."

Hawkins goes on to say :—

" There is a tradition that his death was occasioned by a cold which he caught in the night waiting for admittance to his own house. It is said that he used to keep late hours, and that his wife had given orders to his servants not to let him in after midnight; unfortunately he came home heated with wine from the tavern at an hour later than that prescribed him, and through the inclemency of the air contracted a disorder of which he died. If this be true, it reflects but little honour on Madam Purcell, for so she is styled in the advertisements of his works; and but ill agrees

with those expressions of grief for her dear, lamented
husband, which she makes use of to Lady Howard
in the dedication of the *Orpheus Britannicus*.   It
seems probable that the disease of which he died
was rather a lingering than an acute one, perhaps a
consumption."

We see from this, that Hawkins had some doubt as
to the truth of the story, and his daughter writing in
1822,[1] respecting some aspersions which had been cast
on her mother in reference to her treatment of her
father, says, " Sir John Hawkins was not at home at
all the sooner for his wife's fetching him.   Mrs. Purcell,
I should conjecture, had other modes of attracting
Mr. Purcell; yet *perhaps the whole may have been
as gross a falsification as that* by which Lady Hawkins
is vilified."

In a volume of poetry of glees published by Richard
Clark in 1824, he improves the tale told by Hawkins,
and boldly adds details.   He prints the words of the
catch, " Jack, thou'rt a toper."

> " Jack, thou'rt a toper; let's have t'other quart.
> Ring, we're so sober 'twere a shame to part;
> None but a cuckold bully'd, by his wife
> For coming late, fears a domestic strife;
> I'm free, and so are you! to call and knock
> Boldly, the watchman cries, ' Past two o'clock.' "

To these lines he appends the name of Tom Brown,
and tells us that *Jack* was intended for Dr. Blow,
and that " Purcell appears to have spent much of his
time with Tom Brown, who wrote the words of most

---

[1] *Anecdotes, Biographical Sketches,* by Letitia Matilda Hawkins.

of his catches." Purcell never set a single line of
Brown's, and they were wholly unacquainted with
each other, as may be learnt from the following
verses written by Brown in June, 1693, two years
before Purcell's death, "To his unknown friend, Mr.
H. Purcell, upon his excellent compositions in the
Harmonia Sacra."

> "Long did dark Ignorance our Isle 'ore-spread,
> Our Musick and our Poetry lay dead ;
> But the dull Malice of a barbarous age
> Fell most severe on *David's* sacred page :
> To wound his Sense and quench his Heav'n born fire
> Three vile Translators lewdly did conspire ;
> In holy Doggerel and low chiming Prose
> The King and Poet they at once depose :
> Vainly the unrighteous charge he did bemoan,
> And languish'd in strange numbers, not his own.
> Nor stopt his Usage here ;
> For what escap'd in Wisdom's ancient Rhimes
> Was murder'd o're and o're in the Composer's Chimes.
> What praises *Purcell* to thy Skill are due,
> Who hast to Judah's Monarch been so true ?
> By thee he moves our Hearts, by thee he reigns,
> By thee shakes off the old inglorious Chains,
> And sees new Honours done to his immortal strains.
> Not *Italy,* the Mother of each Art,
> Did e're a juster, happier Son impart.
> In thy performance we with wonder find
> *Corelli's* genius to *Bassani's* join'd.
> Sweetness, combined with Majesty, prepares
> To sing Devotion with inspiring airs.
> Thus I, unknown, my Gratitude express
> And conscious Gratitude could do no less.
> This Tribute from each *British* Muse is due ;
> The whole Poetic Tribe's obliged to you ;
> For when the Author's scanty Words have fail'd,
> Thy happier Graces, *Purcell,* have prevail'd !
> And surely none but you with equal ease,
> Cou'd add to David, and make D'Urfy please."

The above lines were printed in the *Gentleman's*

Journal with an editorial note : "A music book in-
tituled *Harmonia Sacra* will shortly be printed for Mr.
Playford. I need not say anything more to recommend it to you, than that you will find in it many of
Mr. *Henry Purcell's* admirable composures. As they
charm all men, they are universally extolled, and even
those who know him no otherwise than by his Notes
are fond of expressing their sense of his merit. *Mr.
Thomas Brown* is one of those, as you will find by
these lines."

The lines appeared in the several editions of *Harmonia
Sacra* even as late as 1714, and there is no ground for
believing that the poet and musician ever met.

Dr. Arne gave a concert at Drury Lane Theatre on
the 21st of June, 1768, for which he published a book
of the words; and one of the pieces is Purcell's catch,
"Jack, thou'rt a toper." To this Arne has appended the
following note :—

"The words of this catch are said to be written by
Mr. Purcell, wherein, it is obvious, that he meant
no elegance with regard to the poetry; but made it
intirely subservient to his extream pretty design in
the music."

The catch, as has been noticed previously, forms a
part of the opera *Bonduca.*

When we consider the immense amount and varied
kind of labour Purcell accomplished during his short
life of thirty-seven years, we must conclude that although
of a bright and joyous nature he was of temperate
habits ; he had not only his duties at Westminster Abbey

and the Chapel Royal to fulfil, but there was also constant occupation in composing for the Church, the Court, and the Theatre; he had numerous professional pupils, and gave lessons in the families of some of the most distinguished gentry and aristocracy; he also was frequently called upon to preside over and direct the concerts which were given in private assemblies. The Lord Keeper North, well known for his theoretical and practical skill in music, and the author of the *Memoires of Musick*, was wont to employ him in that capacity at his house in Queen Street.

The position Purcell held in his profession necessitated his keeping late hours, which undoubtedly overtaxed a delicate constitution and culminated in his fatal illness in the prime of his manhood. Valuable testimony to this view of the circumstances attending Purcell's death is to be found in a curious volume called the *Great Abuse of Musick*, published in 1711 by the Rev. Arthur Bedford, Chaplain to the Duke of Bedford, and Vicar of the Temple in Bristol. The author, himself a musician and composer, was also the writer of a companion volume, *On the Evil and Danger of Stage Plays*, and in both books he vigorously exposes the vice and immorality prevalent in his day, and is justly severe on poets and musicians; therefore the passages in which he speaks of his contemporaries, Blow and Purcell, are of great importance. He says:—

"It must be confess'd, that whilst musick was chiefly employ'd in the nation for the glory of God, God was pleas'd to shew his approbation thereof by wonderfully improving the skill of the composers, insomuch that

I believe no Art was advanced from so mean a beginning to so vast a height in so short a time as the Science in the last century. Our musick began to equal that of the Italians and to exceed all other. *Our Purcell was the delight of the nation and the wonder of the world,* and the character of Dr. Blow was but little inferior to him. But when we made not that use thereof which we ought, it pleas'd God to shew his resentment, and a stop to our progress by taking away our Purcell in the prime of his age, and Dr. Blow soon after. We all lamented our misfortunes, but never considered them as judgements for the abuse of this science, so that instead of growing better we grew worse and worse. Now, therefore, musick declines as fast as it did improve before."

This testimony respecting Purcell, from a contemporary, a distinguished divine and musician, ought surely to wipe out the preposterous stories of Purcell's cold-catching and low associations.

Valuable testimony to Purcell's high aims and laborious life is to be found in the MSS. written by Dr. Tudway for Edward, Lord Harley, and now deposited in the British Museum. Dr. Tudway was just two years older than Purcell, so that he entered the choir of the Chapel Royal first; he afterwards became a tenor singer in St. George's Chapel, Windsor, and in 1670 organist of King's College, Cambridge, where he afterwards took successively the degrees of Bachelor and Doctor in Music, and eventually became Professor of the University. He was also appointed "composer extraordinary" to Queen Anne. Writing of Purcell, his fellow-student, he says :—

"I knew him perfectly well. He had a most commendable ambition of exceeding every one of his time, and he succeeded in it without contradiction, there being none in England, nor anywhere else that I know of, that could come in competition with him for compositions of all kinds. Towards the latter end of his life he was prevailed on to compose for the English stage. There was nothing that ever had appeared in England like the representations he made of all kinds, whether for pomp or solemnity, in his grand chorus, &c., or that exquisite piece called the freezing piece of musick; in representing a mad couple, or country swains making love, or indeed any other kind of musick whatever. But these are trifles in comparison of the solemn pieces he made for the Church, in which I will name but one, and that is his *Te Deum*, &c., with instruments, a composition for skill and invention beyond what was ever attempted in England before his time."

Evidence respecting Purcell's personal virtues and gifts is to be found in an ode printed at the commencement of the second volume of *Orpheus Britannicus*, 1702. The poem is too long to quote entire, but the following extracts will suffice : —

"Make room ye happy natures of the sky,
Room for a soul, all Love and Harmony ;
A Soul that rose to such Perfection here,
It scarce will be advanced by being there.
Whether (to us by Transmigration given),
He once was an Inhabitant of Heav'n,
And form'd for Musick, with Diviner fire
Endu'd, compos'd, for the Celestial Choir ;
Not for the Vulgar Race of Light to hear,
But on High-days to glad th' Immortal Ear.
So in some leisure hour was sent away,
(Their Hour is here a Life, a Thousand years their Day.)

And what th' Ætherial Musick was to show,
And teach the wonders of that Art below ;
Whether this might not be, the Muse appeals
To his Composures, where such Magick dwells,
As rivals Heav'nly Skill, and human Pow'r excels.

    *   *   *   *

Ah, most unworthy ! shou'd we leave unsung
Such wondrous Goodness in a Life so young.
In spight of Practice, he this Truth hath shown,
That Harmony and Vertue shou'd be one.
So true to Nature, and so just to Wit,
His Musick was the very Sense you Writ.
Nor were his Beauties to his Art confin'd ;
So justly were his Soul and Body join'd,
You'd think his Form the Product of his Mind.
A conqu'ring sweetness in his Visage dwelt,
His Eyes would warm, his Wit like lightning melt.
But those must no more be seen, and that no more be felt.
Pride was the sole aversion of his Eye,
Himself as Humble as his Art was High.
Oh ! let him Heav'n (in Life so much ador'd)
Be now as universally Deplor'd !

    *   *   *   *

There rest thy Ashes—but thy nobler name
Shall soar aloft and last as long as fame.
Nor shall thy Worth be to our Isle confin'd,
But flie and leave the lagging day behind.
Rome, that did once extend its arms so far,
Y'ave conquer'd in a nobler Art than War ;
To its proud Sons but only Earth was giv'n,
But thou hast triumph'd both in Earth and Heav'n."

Purcell's friend and fellow-student, Henry Hall, organist of Hereford Cathedral, also printed an ode "To the Memory of my Dear Friend Mr. Henry Purcell," which concludes thus :—

    " Hail ! and for ever hail, Harmonious shade,
     I lov'd thee living, and admire thee Dead.
     Apollo's harp at once our souls did strike ;
     We learnt together, but not learnt alike :
     Though equal care our Master might bestow,

Yet only Purcell e're shall equal Blow :
For thou by Heaven for wondrous things design'd
Left'st thy companion lagging far behind.
Sometimes a Hero in an age appears,
But once a Purcell in a Thousand Years."

It is clear that Purcell attained the highest pinnacle
in the estimation of his countrymen; [1] but his fame
was not confined to England. I have seen a MS. volume
of music written by a contemporary musician, a native
of France, and in it he designates Purcell as M. Pourselle.
Roger of Amsterdam engraved and printed a set of his
Sonatas; and the following anecdote is told in some of
the biographies of Corelli :—

" While Corelli flourished with such *éclat* at Rome,
Harry Purcell was famous in England, and Corelli was
so greatly affected with the character and abilities of
this famous English musician, that, as fame reports, he
declared him to be then the only thing worth seeing in
England. Accordingly the great opinion he held of
Purcell made him resolve to make a journey into this
kingdom on purpose to visit him," but the journey was
abandoned on hearing of Purcell's death.

Another version of the story makes Corelli start on
his journey, but hearing of Purcell's death on ship-
board, when nearing Dover, he returns immediately to
Rome.

[1] " The English affect more the Italian than the French music,
and their own compositions are between the gravity of the
first and the levity of the other. They have had several
great masters of their own. *Henry Purcell's* works in that
kind are esteemed beyond *Lully's* everywhere, and they have
now a good many very eminent masters ; but the taste of the
town being at this day all Italian, it is a great discouragement
to them."—*Mackay's Journey Through England,* 1722—3.

G

Purcell's secular music undoubtedly frequently suffered from the worthless trash he had to accept as poetry ; too often it was not only devoid of literary merit, but still worse, indecent ; that was, however, the fault of the age, and pervaded most of the dramatic literature then in vogue.   Even the well-known and estimable Dean of Christ Church, Oxford, Dr. Aldrich, condescended to set music to such words as shame would not permit us to print at this day.

Tom D'Urfey was a notorious offender against good taste, and for him Purcell composed very largely.

> " Oh ! who can view without a tear
> Great Pindar's muse and D'Urfey near ?
> Whose soaring wit ne'er higher flew
> Than to endite for Barthol'mew,
> Setting, for sots at country fairs,
> Dull saucy songs to *Purcell's* airs." [1]

D'Urfey's verses were so uncouth and irregular in their construction, that a writer of the last century said, " The modern Pindaric Odes which are humorously resembled to a comb with the teeth broken by frequent use are nothing to them."   D'Urfey wrote some especially rugged lines which he challenged Purcell to set to music ; the challenge was accepted and the composer triumphed, but he confessed that it cost him more trouble than the composition of a *Te Deum*.   The ballad in question was called " The Parson among the Peas," and was printed with Purcell's music in D'Urfey's *Pills to Purge Melancholy*, 1719.

At the present day music has become such an exten-

---

[1] Dr. King's *Bibliotheca,* 1712.

sively developed science, particularly as regards orchestration, that it is difficult to apprehend the state of
things which existed in Purcell's time; but to estimate
his genius fairly we must recall the condition of the
musical artistic world in which he lived. In so far as
orchestration is concerned he had no models, nor had he
any instrumental performers to suggest or incite his
creative powers. Purcell was familiar with the family
of stringed instruments called viols, and although
Charles II. introduced violins from France, yet the
instrument was not regarded with favour by musicians or
by the people generally. Doubtless this arose from the
fact that there were no remarkable players. Anthony
Wood of Oxford, speaking of the year 1657, says :—

"Gentlemen in private meetings, which A. W. fre-
quented, played three, four, and five parts with viols—
as treble viol, tenor, counter-tenor and bass, with an
organ, virginal or harpsicon joined to them; and they
esteemed a *violin* to be an instrument only belonging to
a *common* fiddler, and could not endure that it should
come among them, for feare of making these meetings
to be vain and fiddling."

The first musician to introduce violin playing
proper was Thomas Baltzar, who played at Oxford in
1658, and A. W. "saw him run up his fingers to the
end of the finger-board of the violin, and run them
back insensibly, and all with great alacrity and *very
good tune,* which he nor any one in England saw the
like before."

He also was the first to exhibit in England the
practice of shifting, or the whole shift on the violin,

and the half shift was not introduced until about
1714. Baltzar died in 1663, so that it is not probable
Purcell ever heard him play; indeed it has been justly
remarked that the probability is he never heard a
great violinist. Corelli's works were not introduced
into England until after Purcell's death, and the only
violin music Purcell knew was that composed by
Bassani.

In 1773 Daines Barrington, a well-known writer,
speaks of the "Amazing improvements in execution
which both singers and players have arrived at within
the last fifty years. When Corelli's music was first
published, our ablest violinists conceived that it was
too difficult to be performed. It is now, however,
the first composition attempted by a scholar. Every
year now produces greater and greater prodigies on
other instruments in point of execution."

Wind instruments were equally wanting if we except
the trumpet, hautboy and bassoon, and only the former
could be said to have arrived at any excellence in performance: there were no flutes,[1] clarinets, horns, or
trombones. It cannot therefore be expected that grand
orchestral effects will be found in Purcell's music, but
what we do discover is an amazing comprehension of
the precise sentiment and feeling required by the words
or by the situation; harmonies which surprise us by
their beauty and boldness (many of them must have
been absolutely new when they were created by
Purcell), exquisite and refined melody, true rhythm,

[1] The flute of Purcell's day was blown at the extreme end like
a flageolet, the modern *flauto traverso* was unknown.

and just accent. And when we look at Purcell's purely
instrumental music, his sonatas, we find that as music
they are superior to Corelli—containing more learning,
more ingenuity, and yet without any appearance of
labour or restraint; but Corelli was a violinist, and in
that respect he had the advantage of Purcell, and knew
what passages were best adapted for the instruments for
which he wrote.

Of Purcell's contrapuntal skill it would be im-
possible to speak too highly; he has left for our wonder
and admiration numerous canons constructed in all the
many and artful modes that species of composition is
capable of; the ingenuity and contrivance exhibited give
ample evidence of his diligence and laborious study, and
the highest praise of all is that in spite of the deep
learning of which they give evidence they move as
melodiously, and as freely, as if they were unfettered
by the stern and inflexible chains imposed by the
rules of the schools.

Purcell's weakness in accepting the prevailing taste
for endless " graces " and divisions has already been
adverted to. Another peculiarity which characterises his
music may possibly be accounted for by the statement
by Stafford Smith that " Mr. Purcell has been heard
to declare more than once, that the *variety* which
the *minor* key is capable of affording by the change of
sounds in the ascending and descending scales, induced
him so frequently to give it the preference." [1] Now-a-
days few composers would select the *minor* mode when

---

[1] Stafford Smith's *Collection of English Songs*, 1779.

composing music to the joyful words of the " Gloria Patri," or to the lines,—

> " In these delightful pleasant groves
> Let us celebrate our happy loves."

Yet Purcell did so with perfect success, as his music witnesses.

Very little has been said in the progress of this biography of Purcell's anthems; they are easily obtainable in the fine edition published with so much enthusiasm by Vincent Novello, and in themselves form a most valuable material for study. It is to be hoped that before many years have passed away equal facilities will exist for gaining an intimate knowledge of his chamber and dramatic music.

Purcell's seeming repugnance to the publication of his own music is remarkable. After his death his widow issued the following advertisement :—

" All the excellent compositions of Mr. Henry Purcell, both vocal and instrumental, that have been published, viz. :—

" *His First Book of Twelve Sonatas*, in four parts.

" *His Ayrs and Sonatas*, newly printed in four parts.

" *The Opera of Diocletian.*

" *Te Deum and Jubilate in Score.*

" *A Choice Collection of Lessons*, for the Harpsichord or Spinett, with instructions for beginners.

" These six printed for Madam Purcell, and sold for her by Henry Playford."

This list as already shown is not quite complete

Henry Purcell published an *Ode for Cecilia's Day*, in 1684, and the *Songs in the Fairy Queen*, in 1692. What a meagre selection from the catalogue of his known works, which numbered nearly 150 sacred compositions, and nearly 50 dramatic compilations, 28 odes, and a large number of other vocal and instrumental pieces which cannot be classed under either of the foregoing heads.

Professor Taylor has eloquently said—

"It would seem as if the view which Purcell had obtained of the powers and resources of his art, and his conviction of what it might hereafter accomplish, had led him to regard all that he had produced but as the efforts of a learner (and we are justified in this conclusion from his own words), fitted to give a brief and transient impulse to his art, and having accomplished this purpose, to be forgotten. It may be that he was right: it may be that we stand, as he stood, but at the threshold of music: it may be that in his 'clear dream and solemn vision' he saw further than his successors: nor will it be denied, that some of its recesses have been further explored by genuises and talent like his own; but all the great attributes which belong to the true artist, all the requirements which make the true musician, we may yet learn of Purcell."

PURCELL'S FAMILY.

IN the foregoing pages I have spoken of Purcell's
father and uncle, but made no mention of his ancestry.
Nothing absolutely certain is known of them. Various
surmises have been made from time to time, and as the
name of Purcel had been common in Ireland for some
centuries,[1] people have endeavoured to trace the composer's family in that country, but no reason or evidence
has as yet been found for supposing that Purcell
inherited Celtic blood.

The national archives preserved at Somerset House
furnish material for speculation in this matter; the
following wills may very probably have been made by
some of the great composer's ancestors:—

"Will proved 1547 8 (fo: 3 Populwell).
DAVJD FYSSHER of Salopp Sherman—
　　to my Kynsman Nicholas pursell
　　to John pursell of Marten, V^{li}.
　　to George pursell, V^{li}.
　　to Thomas purshell, Nicholas sonne, V^{li}.
　　to Roger Calcott of Buttington, Viij^s."

[1] Purcell is named as one of the possessors of property in
a map of Ireland made about the middle of the seventeenth
century.

⁕ Will proved 1547 (43 Alen.)

JOHN FYSSHER, gentⁿ of Hen. VI1., Hen. VIII., and Edw. VI. chapels—

'to my Cosyn,[1] John Pursell, XXˢ sterling, all my londes in Clevedon and Clopton. . . . Countie of Somers nye to Bristowe;' to brother David Fyssher of Shrewsbury for life and after to Cosyn Nicholas pursell and heirs for ever."

The parish registers of St. Margaret's, Westminster, contain occasional mention of the name of Pursell or Purcell, the earliest being 1575; but whether the records before 1658 refer to members of the composer's family it has not been possible to determine.

Purcell's mother died in August, 1699, having survived her son nearly four years; her burial is recorded in the books of St. Margaret's, Westminster, thus:—" Mrs. Elizᵗʰ Purcell, Ch.[2] August 26, 1699;" her estate was "administered to" on the 7th of the following September by her daughter Katherine, who had been baptized in Westminster Abbey on the 13th of March, 1662. This younger sister of Purcell was married on the 20th June, 1691, to the Rev. William Sale, of Sheldwich, Kent.

Purcell had two brothers, Edward and Daniel: the former was born in 1653. The story of his life is briefly told in the inscription placed on his gravestone in the chancel of Wytham Church, near Oxford:

" Here lyeth the body of Edward Purcell, eldest son of Mr. Purcell, gentleman of the Royal Chapel, and

---

[1] Cosyn usually meant nephew.
[2] Meaning buried in the Church.

brother to Mr. Henry Purcell so much renowned for his
skill in musick. He was gentleman usher to King
Charles the 2nd, and lieutenant in Col. Trelawney's
regiment of foot, in which for his many gallant actions
in the wars of Ireland and Flanders he was gradually
advanced to the honour of Lieutenant-colonel. He
assisted Sir George Rook in the taking of Gibraltar, and
the Prince of Hesse in the memorable defence of it.
He followed that Prince to Barcelona, was at the taking
of Mountjoy where that brave Prince was killed; and
continued to signalize his courage in the siege and taking
of the city in the year 1705. He enjoyed the glory of
his great services till the much lamented death of his
late mistress, Queen Anne, when, decayed with age and
broken with misfortunes, he retired to the house of the
Right Hon. Montague, Earl of Abingdon, and died
June 20, 1717, aged 64."

Daniel Purcell was a younger brother of the great
composer; the exact date of his birth is not known, but
it is believed to have been about 1660. Of his early
musical training nothing has been ascertained, he was
too young when his father died to have received any
instructions from him; possibly in his boyhood he may
not have shown remarkable traits of musical ability;
and in his more mature years his undoubted talent was
altogether over-shadowed by the superior genius of his
brother, to whom he was indebted for some part of the
practical and theoretical knowledge of music he possessed.
The first official appointment with which we can identify
him is that of organist of Magdalen College, Oxford,
to which he succeeded in 1686, soon after the ejectment
from that post of Dr. Benjamin Rogers, who with the
other fellows of the College was unjustly expelled by

James II. In 1693 Daniel Purcell composed music for a "Saint Cecilia's Day Ode" written by Thomas Yalden, which is believed to have been performed at Oxford. He resigned his appointment at Magdalen College in 1695, in order that he might reside in London, and in the following year, 1696, composed music for the tragedy "Ibrahim XII.," written by Mary Pix; also for an opera called "Brutus of Alba, or Augusta's Triumph." This was written by George Powell, the comedian, and John Verbruggen; it was performed at the theatre in Dorset Gardens in the following year. The songs were immediately published with a dedication "to P. Norton and A. Henley, Esquires." In 1697, in conjunction with Jeremiah Clarke, he composed music for Settle's opera, "The New World in the Moon," and also for D'Urfey's opera, "Cynthia and Endymion." In 1698 he composed songs for a tragedy, "Phaeton, or the Fatal Divorce," written by Gildon, also an ode for the Princess Anne's birthday,[1] and an ode for Saint Cecilia's Day, written by Bishop.[2] In 1699, he was associated with Jeremiah Clarke and Leveridge in composing music for "The Island Princess," an opera by Motteux, and he also composed music for a "Saint Cecilia Ode" written by Addison for performance at Oxford. In 1700 he composed the work which has generally been considered his greatest success, an opera entitled "The

[1] The autograph score is in the British Museum.
[2] "On Wednesday next will be performed at York Buildings Mr. Daniel Purcell's musick, made for last St. Cecilia's Feast, for the benefit of Mr. Howel and Mr. Shore, with an addition of new vocal and instrumental musick."—*London Gazette,* December 29, 1698.

Grove, or Love's Paradise," written by J. Oldmixon, and performed at Drury Lane. Daniel Purcell is said to have designed and penned this music whilst staying with his patron, Anthony Henley, of the Grange, in Hampshire, or at the residence of Philip Norton, of Southwick, in the same county, another of his patrons, who was in the habit of entertaining his friends in the summer time with dramatic representations.

On the 21st of March, 1699,[1] the following advertisement appeared in the *London Gazette :—*

" Several persons of quality, having for the encouragement of musick advanced 200 guineas, to be distributed in 4 prizes, the first of 100, the second of 50, the third of 30, and the fourth of 20 guineas, to such masters as shall be adjudged to compose the best; this is therefore to give notice, that those who intend to put in for the prizes are to repair to Jacob Tonson at Gray's-Inn Gate, before Easter next day, where they may be further informed."

The Earl of Halifax was the originator and one of the principal contributors to the prize fund; he was also one of the adjudicators. The poem selected for the composers to exercise their skill and fancy on was "The Judgment of Paris," written by Congreve. The first prize was won by John Weldon,[2] the second by John Eccles, *the third by Daniel Purcell,* and the fourth by Godfrey Finger.

The prize compositions of Daniel Purcell and Eccles were speedily published, but Weldon's work remains in

---

[1] 1700 according to the new style.
[2] A pupil of Henry Purcell.

57182

MS., as does also that by Finger, who was so annoyed at the small success his composition achieved that he left England in disgust.

In 1701 Daniel Purcell composed music for "The Unhappy Penitent," a tragedy by Catherine Trotter; in 1702 for "The Inconstant," a comedy by Farquhar. In the *Diverting Post*, October 28th, 1704, we read—

"The Play-house in the Hay-Market (the architect being John Vanbrugh, Esq.), built by the subscription money of most of our Nobility, is almost finish'd : in the meantime two operas, translated from the Italian by good Hands, are setting to musick, one by Mr. Daniel Purcel, which is called 'Orlando Furioso,' and the other by Mr. Clayton : both operas are to be perform'd by the best artists, eminent both for Vocal and Instrumental Musick, at the Opening of the House."

This composition was very highly commended in the *Muses Mercury*, 1707, which speaks also in warm terms of a masque set by Daniel Purcell called "Orpheus and Euridice." In 1707 he composed a "Saint Cecilia Ode," which was performed at Oxford in St. Mary's Hall.

An advertisement in the *Spectator*, No. 340, March 31, 1712, tells us—

"On Wednesday the 3rd of April, at Stationers' Hall, Mr. Daniel Purcell, brother of the memorable Mr. Henry Purcell, will exhibit an entertainment of Vocal and Instrumental Musick entirely new, and all parts to be performed with the greatest excellence."

Amongst his compositions, printed and manuscript, not already mentioned, are Anthems, Songs for the plays

"The Careless Husband," "The Humor of the Age,"
and "Magbeth." [1]   "Sonatas or Solos for the violin with
a thorough bass for the harpsichord, or bass-violin."
"Sonatas for flute and bass," and "A Lamentation for
the Death of Mr. Henry Purcell."

The words of this "Lamentation" were written by
Nahum Tate, and conclude with the following lines :—

> "A sighing Wind, a murm'ring Rill,
> Our Ears with doleful Accents fill :
> They are heard, and only they,
> For sadly thus they seem to say,
> The Joy, the Pride of Spring is Dead,
> The Soul of Harmony is fled.
> Pleasure's flown from Albion's Shore,
> Wit and Mirth's bright Reign is o're,
> Strephon and music are no more !
> Since Nature thus pays Tribute to his Urn,
> How should a sad, forsaken Brother mourn ! "

Daniel Purcell was appointed organist of St. Andrew,
Holborn, in 1713, and retained the position until his
death in 1717.   Sir John Hawkins in his History,[2]
says :—

"The occasion of Daniel Purcell's coming to London
was as follows :—Dr. Sacheverell, who had been a
friend of his brother Henry, having been presented
to the living of St. Andrew, Holborn, found an organ
in the church of Harris's building, which having never
been paid for, had from the time of its erection, in 1699,
been shut up. The Doctor upon his coming to the
living, by a collection from the parishioners, raised

---

[1] " A Song sung by Mr. Mason in *Magbeth*, sett by Mr. D.
Purcell, 'Cease, gentle Swain,' in the Queen's library, Buckingham
Palace."

[2] Vol. ii. p. 759, new Edition.   Novello & Co.

money to pay for it; but the title to the place of organist was litigated, the right of election being in question between the rector, the vestry, and the parish at large. Nevertheless he invited Daniel Purcell to London, and he accepted it; but in February, 1717, the vestry, which in that parish is a select one, thought proper to elect Mr. Maurice Greene, afterwards Dr. Greene, in preference to Purcell, who submitted to stand as a candidate. In the year following Greene was made organist of St. Paul's, and Daniel Purcell being then dead, his nephew Edward was a candidate for the place; but it was conferred on Mr. John Isum, who died in June, 1726."

That Hawkins has made a series of mistakes in the above statement, is clear from the following advertisement, which appeared in the *Daily Courant*, December 12, 1717:—

" Whereas Edward Purcell, only son to the Famous Mr. Henry Purcell, stands candidate for the Organist's place of St. Andrew, Holborn, in the room of his uncle Mr. Daniel Purcell, deceased,—This is to give notice, that the place is to be decided by a general Poll of Housekeepers of the said Parish, whom he humbly hopes, notwithstanding the false and malicious reports of his being a Papist, will be assistant to him in obtaining the said place.

" N.B.—The election will begin upon Tuesday the 17th, at nine in the morning, and continue till Friday following, to four in the afternoon."

This shows that Daniel vacated his organistship by death. Unfortunately the parish book which might tell us the result of the election by the householders cannot be found; but it evidently was not permitted to be a final decision, for on the 17th of the ensuing February, 1718, a Vestry was held, of which the following is a minute :—[1]

"The question being put whether the vestry should take the election of an organist into their nomination, it was agreed in the affirmative.
"The candidates were—

MR. SHORT	.	.	.	.
„ ISHAM	.	.	.	.
„ YOUNG	.	.	.	.
„ GREEN	.	.	.	. //////
„ PURSILL	.	.	.	.
„ HAYDON		.	.	.
„ HARRIS	.	.	.	.
„ HART	.	.	.	.

"Mr. Green is elected Organist of the Parish of St. Andrew, Holborn."

The strokes show that Greene was elected by six votes, seemingly the whole vestry, as no votes are marked against the names of the other candidates. Greene, however, soon resigned the appointment, and a new election took place.

"1718, 3ᵈ of April, Mr. Green yᵉ Organist being elected Organist of St. Paul's and his place as Organist of this Church being become vacant, the Vestry do order his salary be continued to Sunday the 4th of May. It is also ordered that such person who shall be elected Organist of this Parish in the room of

[1] Extracted from the Vestry books of St. Andrew's, Holborn.

Mr. Green, shall be obliged to a constant personall attendance on all Sundays and Holydays.

"The several candidates—

MR. G. HAYDON . . . /
  „ C. YOUNG . . . .
  „ EDWARD PURSIL . .
  „ JOHN ISHAM . . . ///////////

"Agreed that Mr. John Isham be elected Organist of the Parish Church in the room of Mr. Green, and that he have a yearly salary of Fifty pounds payd him out of the Bells and Palls."

Here again Edward Purcell was unsuccessful, Mr. John Isham obtaining eleven votes.

After the death of Daniel Purcell the following advertisement appeared in the *Post Boy*, Saturday, 26th April, 1718:—

"Musick this day published, Being a choice Collection, &c., to which is added all the Psalm tunes by the late Mr. Daniel Purcell."

This work was probably the curious collection still extant bearing the following title: "The Psalms Set full for the Organ or Harpsichord as they are Plaid in Churches and Chappels in the maner given out; as also with their interludes of great Variety, by Mr. Dan¹ Purcell, late Organist of St. Andrew's, Holbourn."

Daniel Purcell is credited by Hawkins as having been more skilful and successful as a punster than as a composer. Of his puns we have now no evidence upon which to form a judgment, but his music exists to show that the historian's verdict is not always to be relied on.

Of the children of Henry Purcell mention has

H

already been made : he had six in all, three of them,
John Baptista, Thomas, and Henry, died in infancy,
during the lifetime of their father; and it is probable that
a fourth child, Mary Peters, survived him but a few
months. The daughter Frances, who was born in 1688,
outlived both her parents; her mother immediately
before her death, in February, 1706, nominated Frances
as her executrix and residuary legatee : accordingly she
proved the will on the 4th July following.   She married
Leonard Welsted, a poet and dramatist, son of the Rev.
Leonard Welsted, Rector of Abington, Northamptonshire.
Welsted had been a King's scholar at Westminster
School, from whence he was elected to Trinity College,
Cambridge. "When very young he married the daughter
of Henry Purcell, the celebrated musician, and obtained
an appointment in the Secretary of State's office." [1]

The young couple were of the same age, and must
have married when nineteen, as the register of St.
Margaret's, Westminster, records the baptism of their
daughter Frances on the 2nd of September, 1708.[2]
Mrs. Welsted died in 1724, not having attained the age
of her celebrated father, and the daughter died in 1726,
aged eighteen.

Purcell's youngest son, Edward, born in 1689, was
the only one who survived him, and like his father, was
but six years old when he became an orphan. His
mother had promised her dying husband carefully to
attend to the child's education, a promise she conscien-

---

[1] Baker's *History of Northamptonshire*, vol. i. p. 17.
[2] "Frances, daughter of Leonard Welsted, Gent, and Frances
his wife."

tiously and affectionately kept for ten years, until 1706, when she died, leaving the lad of sixteen to the guidance of his sister Frances, who was but two years older. The children, however, possessed many influential friends, and in the following year, 1707, Frances married. We know nothing more of Edward's doings for a few succeeding years, but it is probable that he married in 1710, as the register-book of St. Margaret's, Westminster, contains the entry of a baptism on " May 4th, 1711, of Frances, daughter of Edward and Anne Purcell, born on 19th April." The register-book of St. Martin-in-the-Fields for 1716 contains a baptismal entry which seems to refer to a son of Edward Purcell : " Dec. 11, Henry, son of Edward and Anne Purcell, born 26 Nov." In 1717 Edward was a candidate for the organist's place of St. Andrew's, Holborn, as I have shown when speaking of Daniel Purcell ; but Edward was, as we have seen, unsuccessful, not only on that occasion, but also in 1718 when he again applied for the appointment. In 1726, on the 8th of July, he was made organist of St. Margaret's, Westminster, and it is said that he succeeded his father as organist of St. Clement's, Eastcheap. In 1738 he was enrolled amongst the first list of members and founders of the " Society of Musicians," now known as the " Royal Society of Musicians," and it is supposed that he died in 1740, as in that year he ceased to be organist of St. Margaret's, Westminster. His successor was appointed on the 6th of August, 1740.

He had a son, the date of whose birth I have not been able to trace, who was named *Edward Henry*.

Hawkins blunders here again : he says Edward Purcell
"was succeeded by his son Henry, who had been bred
up in the King's Chapel under Mr. Gates. This Henry
became also organist of St. Edmund the King, London,
and after that of St. John, Hackney. He died about
twenty-five years ago.[1] His father was a good organist,
but himself a very indifferent one."

The statement is brimful of errors, as we shall see.

Chamberlaine's *Magnœ Britannia Notitia,* 1737, on
page 219, gives the "children's names" of the Chapel
Royal,[2] and there we find *Edward Henry Purcell.* The
correctness of the name is confirmed by an entry in a
magnificent book of music now in the Queen's library
in Buckingham Palace. The volume is wholly in Henry
Purcell's autograph. It had belonged to Edward Purcell,
and contains an entry in his hand : "Score booke—
Anthems and Welcome Songs, and other songs, all by
my father." At the other end of the book is an autograph
inscription, "Ed H. Purcell, Grandson to the Author
of this book."

In 1753, August 11th, the vestry of St. John, Hackney,

" Resolved and agreed that ye place of organist of the
Parish be and is declared vacant ; agreed that the sallary
of ye organist of the Parish be settled.

" Organist his duty.—That the salary of the organist
shall for the future be £20 by the year, and that for his
said salary he shall attend all Sundays in the year, and
on all days whenever a sermon shall be preached, Fast-
days excepted, and that on every Sunday throughout the
year a voluntary shall be played after both morning and
evening service."

[1] 1750.   [2] The master was Bernard Gates.

"Ordered, that an advertisement be published in the paper called the *Daily Advertiser*, that the place of Organist of this Parish is vacant, and that all persons who are willing to be candidates for the same may apply to Mr. Ch.-warden Barnard."

"On the 22nd Sept., 1753, the candidates appeared separately before the Vestry, ' and a Vestry was held to choose an organist.' Candidates being—

MR. EDWARD HENRY PURCELL . .	9	Votes.
MR. DAVID L. HEUREUX. . . .	6	„
MR. WILLIAM WARD	2	„
MR. RICHARD LOW	0	„
MR. THOMAS ARCHER	1	„
MR. MOSES PATENCE	0	„

"The majority being for Mr. Ed. Hen. Purcell, he was declared Organist of this Parish till Easter next."

The parish books show that he was re-elected annually down to Easter Tuesday, April 24, 1764, when there is an entry—

"Complaint having been made against Edward Henry Purcell the present organist. Resolved—That the Vestry Clerk do write to the said Edward Henry Purcell and acquaint him that the Vestry insists on his being regular in his attendance, and that he do give in the name of his Deputy to the Churchwardens, and also give notice from time to time to the Churchwardens for the time being when he shall charge him and who he shall appoint in his stead."

"April 30, 1764. The Vestry Clerk acquainted the Vestry that he had wrote to Mr. Purcell the Organist agreeable to the Resolution of the last Vestry. Resolved that the choice of an organist be deferred until the next Vestry and that Mr. Purcell do officiate in the meantime."

There is also an entry made by the Vestry Clerk, April, 1764 : "N.B.—Wrote to him and he said he would name his deputy."

On Easter Tuesday, April 8th, 1765, the Vestry minutes record the appointment of organ-blower, but no mention is made of the organist; we may therefore infer that Purcell was not continued in the post, as in the following year, 1766, we read—

"Resolved that David Ld Heureux organist, Sarah Palmer organ-blower, Be and they are hereby continued in their respective offices at their annual Sallarys until Easter Tuesday next."

ORGANISTS OF WESTMINSTER ABBEY.

NAME	DATE
John Howe	1549
Master Whitt	1560
John Taylor	1562
Robert White	1570
Henry Leeve	1575
Edmund Hooper, the first regular appointment as Organist	1588
John Parsons	1621
Orlando Gibbons	1623
Thomas Day	1625
Richard Portman	1633
Christopher Gibbons	1660
Albertus Bryne	1666
John Blow	1669
Henry Purcell	1680
John Blow	1695
William Croft	1708
John Robinson	1727
Benjamin Cooke	1762
Samuel Arnold	1794
Robert Cooke	1803
George Ebenezer Williams	1815
Thomas Greatorex	1819
James Turle	1831
J. Frederick Bridge	1882

MASTERS OF THE CHORISTER BOYS OF WESTMINSTER ABBEY.

NAME	DATE
John Taylor	1562
Robert White	1574
Henry Leeve	1575
Edmund Hooper	1585
John Gibbs	1605

NAME	DATE.
John Parsons	1613
Thomas Day	1623
Richard Portman	1633
James Trye	1637
Walter Porter	1639
Henry Purcell (senior)	1661
Christopher Gibbons	1664
Thomas Blagrave	1666
Edward Braddock	1670
John Church	1704
Bernard Gates	1740

MUSIC COPYISTS OF WESTMINSTER ABBEY.

NAME	DATE.
Henry Purcell (senior)	1661
Christopher Gibbons	1664
Stephen Byng	1673
Henry Purcell (junior)	1676
William Tucker	1678
Charles Taylour	1684
Henry Purcell	1688
Edward Braddock	1690
John Church	1710
John Buswell	1761
Thomas Vanderman	1763
Thomas Barrow	1782

CHRONOLOGICAL MEMORANDA.

1658. Henry Purcell, the composer, born.

1659. Meeting of Purcell's father, Matthew Locke, and Pepys.

1661. Charles the Second crowned. Henry Purcell, the father, and Thomas Purcell, the uncle of the composer, attend the coronation as gentlemen of the Chapel Royal.

1663. Purcell's father appointed a member of the Royal Band.

1664. The father died. Purcell entered the Chapel Royal under Captain Cooke.

1667. Purcell's three-part song, "Sweet Tyraness," published.

1669. Purcell composed "An Address to the King."

1672. Purcell's master, Captain Cooke, died; succeeded by Pelham Humphreys.

1674. Humphreys died; succeeded by Dr. John Blow.

1676. Purcell appointed copyist of Westminster Abbey. Composed music for (1) "Epsom Wells;" (2) "Aurenge-Zebe; (3) "The Libertine."

1677. Purcell composed an Elegy on the death of Matthew Locke; also the music for "Abdelazor."

1678. Resigned the appointment of copyist at Westminster Abbey. "Sweet Tyraness," newly arranged, republished. Music for "Timon of Athens" composed.

1679. Composed music for Rev. John Gostling's voice.

1680. Appointed organist of Westminster Abbey. Composed music for (1) "The Virtuous Wife;" (2) "Theodosius;" and the Opera "Dido and Æneas." Also two Odes, "A welcome song for his Royal Highness's return from Scotland," and "A song to welcome his Majesty home from Windsor."

1681. Composed an Ode for the King, "Swifter, Isis, swifter flow."

1682. Purcell appointed organist of the Chapel Royal. Composed an Ode for the King "On his return from Newmarket;" also music for "The Lord Mayor's Show." His uncle Thomas died; a son, John Baptista, born and died.

1683. Sonatas of three parts published. Appointed "composer in ordinary" to the King. Composed three Odes for the festival of St. Cecilia;" also "A welcome song

for the King ; " " Fly, bold rebellion ; " and Ode, " From
hardy climes," for Prince George of Denmark, on his
marriage with the Princess Anne.

1684. Published a " St. Cecilia" Ode. Composed an Ode to welcome the King, " On his return to Whitehall after his
summer's progress." Performed on the new organ
erected by Father Smith in the Temple Church.

1685. James II. crowned in Westminster Abbey. For the ceremony Purcell composed two Anthems, " I was glad,"
and " My heart is inditing." Composed an Ode, " Why
are all the muses mute," in honour of the King. Also
the music for " Circe."

1686. Composed " Lilliburlero," also the music for " Tyrannic
Love." His brother and pupil, Daniel, appointed organist
of Magdalen College, Oxford. His infant son, Thomas,
died. An Ode for the King, " Ye tuneful muses,"
composed.

1687. Composed an Elegy on the death of John Playford, the
younger. An Ode for the King, " Sound the trumpet,
beat the drum." Purcell's son, Henry, born and died.

1688. Purcell composed, by command, a thanksgiving Anthem
for the Queen's pregnancy, " Blessed are they that fear
the Lord." Composed also the music for " A fool's
preferment," an Ode " For the King," and the Anthem,
" The Lord is King." A daughter, Frances, born.

1689. William and Mary crowned in Westminster Abbey. Purcell
threatened, by Dean and Chapter of Westminster, with
suspension. Composed " Celestial music" an Ode " At
the Prince of Denmark's coming home," also " The
Yorkshire feast song." A son, Edward, born.

1690. Purcell composed an Ode, " Arise my muse," for the
Queen's birthday, and another, " Sound the trumpet,"
for King William. Also music for (1) " The Tempest ; "
(2) " Dioclesian ; " (3) " Massacre of Paris ; " (4)
" Amphitryon."

1691. He composed music for (1) " Distressed innocence ; " (2)
" King Arthur ; " (3) " The Gordian knot untyed ; "
(4) " Sir Anthony Love ; " also an Ode, " Welcome,
glorious morn," for the Queen's birthday.

1692. He composed the music for (1) " The Fairy Queen " (and
published " Some select songs " from that opera); (2)
" The Wife's excuse ; " (3) " The Indian Queen ; " (4)
" The Indian Emperour ; " (5) " Œdipus ; " (6) " Cleo-
menes ; " (7) " The marriage-hater match'd ; " also an
Ode, " Love's goddess sure was blind," for the Queen's

birthday, and an Ode, "Hail, great Cecilia," for the anniversary of St. Cecilia.

1693. He composed a Commemoration Ode, "Great Parent, hail," for Trinity College, Dublin, and music for (1) "The old bachelor;" (2) "The Richmond heiress;" (3) "The maid's last prayer;" (4) "Henry the Second." Also an Ode, "Celebrate this festival," for the Queen's birthday.

1694. He composed music for the first and second parts of (1) "Don Quixote;" (2) "The married beau;" (3) "The double dealer;" (4) "The fatal marriage;" (5) "Love triumphant;" also the Te Deum and Jubilate in D for the festival of St. Cecilia, and an Ode, "Come, ye sons of art," for the Queen's birthday. "The art of descant," for John Playford.

1695. He composed Anthems for the funeral of Queen Mary, "Blessed is the man," and "Thou knowest, Lord." Two Latin Elegies on the Queen. A birthday Ode, "Who can from joy refrain?" for the Duke of Gloucester. Music for (1) "The Canterbury Guests;" (2) "The Mock Marriage;" (3) "The Rival Sisters;" (4) "Oroonoko;" (5) "The Knight of Malta;" (6) "Bonduca;" (7) "The third part of Don Quixote." Purcell died Nov. 21st; buried in Westminster Abbey, Nov. 26th.

1699. Purcell's mother died.

1706. Purcell's widow died.

1707. Purcell's daughter married to L. Welsted.

1710. Purcell's son, Edward, married.

1717. Edward Purcell and Daniel Purcell, the composer's brothers, died.

1726. Purcell's son, Edward, organist of St. Margaret's, Westminster.

1737. Edward Henry Purcell, grandson of the composer, a child of the Chapel Royal.

1738. Purcell's son, Edward, organist of St. Margaret's, Westminster.

1740. Edward died.

1753. Edward Henry Purcell, grandson of the composer organist of St. John, Hackney.

1765. Not re-elected to St. John, Hackney.

INDEX.

THE END.